P9-CQW-841

A POWER
governments cannot suppress

306. 20973
Zinn. H

Original Zinn: Conversations on History and Politics, with David Barsamian (HarperCollins/ Perennial, 2006).

A People's History of the United States: 1492–Present, updated ed. (HarperCollins/Perennial, 2005).

The People Speak: American Voices, Some Famous, Some Little Known (HarperCollins/Perennial, 2006).

Voices of a People's History of the United States, with Anthony Arnove (Seven Stories Press, 2004).

Artists in Times of War (Seven Stories Press/Open Media Series, 2003).

Passionate Declarations: Essays on War and Justice (Harper/Perennial, 2003).

You Can't Be Neutral on a Moving Train: A Personal History of Our Times, 2d ed. (Beacon Press, 2002).

Terrorism and War, with Anthony Arnove (Seven Stories Press/Open Media Series, 2002).

Emma (South End Press, 2002).

Three Strikes: Miners, Musicians, Salesgirls, and the Fighting Spirit of Labor's Last Century, with Dana Frank and Robin D. G. Kelley (Beacon Press, 2001).

Howard Zinn on War (Seven Stories Press, 2001).

Howard Zinn on History (Seven Stories Press, 2001).

La otra historia de los Estados Unidos (Seven Stories Press, 2001).

Marx in Soho: A Play on History (South End Press, 1999).

The Future of History: Interviews with David Barsamian (Common Courage Press, 1999).

The Zinn Reader: Writings on Disobedience and Democracy (Seven Stories Press, 1997).

Failure to Quit: Reflections of an Optimistic Historian (Common Courage Press, 1993; rpt. ed. South End Press, 2002).

The Politics of History, 2nd ed. (University of Illinois, 1990).

Justice: Eyewitness Accounts (Beacon Press, 1977; rpt. ed. South End Press, 2002).

Postwar America: 1945–1971 (Bobbs-Merrill, 1973; rpt. ed. South End Press, 2002).

Disobedience and Democracy: Nine Fallacies of Law and Order (Vintage, 1968; rpt. ed. South End Press, 2002).

Vietnam: The Logic of Withdrawal (Beacon Press, 1967; rpt. ed. South End Press, 2002).

(Ed.) *New Deal Thought* (Bobbs-Merrill, 1966).

SNCC: The New Abolitionists (Beacon Press, 1964; rpt. ed. South End Press, 2002).

The Southern Mystique (Knopf, 1964; rpt. ed. South End Press, 2002).

LaGuardia in Congress (Cornell University, 1959).

A POWER
governments cannot suppress

HOWARD ZINN

City Lights Books
San Francisco

Copyright © 2007 by Howard Zinn

All Rights Reserved

For permissions information see page 271.

Cover photograph of the Selma to Montgomery March, March 21–25, 1965, by James Karales.

Back cover photograph of Howard Zinn by Robert Birnbaum.

Cover design by Pollen, New York.

Book design by Gambrinus.

Library of Congress Cataloging-in-Publication Data

Zinn, Howard, 1922-
    A power governments cannot suppress / Howard Zinn.
       p. cm.
    Includes bibliographical references and index.
    ISBN-13: 978-0-87286-475-7 (pbk.)
    ISBN-10: 0-87286-475-8 (pbk.)
    ISBN-13: 978-0-87286-455-9 (cloth)
    ISBN-10: 0-87286-455-3 (cloth)
    1. United States—History. 2. United States—Politics and
government. 3. United States—Politics and government—
Philosophy. 4. Democracy—United States. 5. Political participation—United States. 6. United States—Social conditions.
I. Title.
  E178.6.Z56 2006
  306.20973—dc22

                                              2006024087

City Lights Books are published at the City Lights Bookstore,
261 Columbus Avenue, San Francisco, CA 94133.

Visit our Web site: www.citylights.com

While there is a lower class, I am in it; while there is a criminal element, I am of it; while there is a soul in prison, I am not free.

—EUGENE DEBS

When the subject has refused allegiance, and the officer has resigned his office, then the revolution is accomplished.

—HENRY DAVID THOREAU

But remember always, Dante, in this play of happiness, don't you use all for yourself only . . . help the persecuted and the victim because they are your better friends. . . . In this struggle of life you will find more love and you will be loved.

—NICOLA SACCO

ACKNOWLEDGMENTS

Thanks to Matt Rothschild, editor of the *Progressive*, for generously allowing use of the columns I wrote for him these past several years.

I also thank Greg Ruggiero, my editor, who initiated the idea of this collection and put great effort into choosing and pruning, right up to publication.

And thanks to City Lights Books, whose history is a distinguished one, and with whom I am proud to publish.

CONTENTS

IF HISTORY IS TO BE CREATIVE

America's future is linked to how we understand our past. For this reason, writing about history, for me, is never a neutral act. By writing, I hope to awaken a great consciousness of racial injustice, sexual bias, class inequality, and national hubris. I also want to bring into the light the unreported resistance of people against the power of the Establishment: the refusal of the indigenous to simply disappear; the rebellion of black people in the antislavery movement and in the more recent movement against racial segregation; the strikes carried out by working people all through American history in attempts to improve their lives.

To omit these acts of resistance is to support the official view that power only rests with those who have the guns and possess the wealth. I write in order to illustrate the creative power of people struggling for a better world. People, when organized, have enormous power, more than any government. Our history runs deep with the stories of people who stand up, speak out, dig in, organize, connect, form networks of resistance, and alter the course of history.

I don't want to invent victories for people's movements. But to think that history writing must aim simply to recapitulate the failures that dominate the past is to make historians collaborators in an endless cycle of defeat. If history is to be creative, to anticipate a possible future without denying the past, it should, I believe, emphasize new possibilities by disclosing those hidden episodes of the past when, even if in brief flashes, people showed their ability to resist, to join together, and occasionally to win. I am supposing, or perhaps only hoping, that our future may be found in the past's fugitive moments of compassion rather than in its solid centuries of warfare.

History can help our struggles, if not conclusively, then at least suggestively. History can disabuse us of the idea that the government's interests and the people's interests are the same.

History can tell how often governments have lied to us, how they have ordered whole populations to be massacred, how they deny the existence of the poor, how they have led us to our current historical moment—the "Long War," the war without end.

True, our government has the power to spend the country's wealth as it wishes. It can send troops anywhere in the world. It can threaten indefinite detention and deportation of 20 million immigrant Americans who do not yet have green cards and have no constitutional rights. In the name of our "national interest," the government can deploy troops to the U.S.-Mexican border, round up Muslim men from certain countries, secretly listen in on our conversations, open our e-mails, examine our bank transactions, and try to intimidate us into silence.

The government can control information with the collaboration of a timid mass media. Only this accounts for the popularity—waning by 2006 (33 percent of those polled), but still significant—of George W. Bush. Still, this control is not absolute. The fact that the media are 95 percent in favor of continuing the occupation of Iraq (with only superficial criticism of how it is done), while more than 50 percent of the public are in favor of withdrawal, suggests a commonsense resistance to official explanations.

Consider also the volatile nature of public opinion, how it can change with dramatic suddenness. Note how the large majority of public support for George Bush the elder quickly collapsed once the glow of victory from the First Gulf War (1990–91) faded and the reality of economic trouble set in.

Think of how, near the start of the Vietnam War in 1965, two-thirds of Americans supported the war. A few years later, two-thirds of Americans opposed the war. What happened in those three or four years? A gradual osmosis of truth seeped through the cracks of the propaganda system— a realization of having been lied to and deceived. That is what is happening in America as I write this in the summer of 2006.

It is easy to be overwhelmed or intimidated by the realization that the war makers have enormous power. But some historical perspective can be useful, because it tells us that at certain points in history governments find that all their power is futile against the power of an aroused citizenry.

There is a basic weakness in governments, however massive their armies, however vast their wealth, however they control images and information, because their power depends on the obedience of citizens, of soldiers, of civil servants, of journalists and writers and teachers and artists. When the citizens begin to suspect they have been deceived and withdraw their support, government loses its legitimacy and its power.

We have seen this happen in recent decades all around the globe. Awaking one morning to see a million angry people in the streets of the capital city, the leaders of a country begin packing their bags and calling for a helicopter.

This is not fantasy; it is recent history. It's the history of the Philippines, of Indonesia, of Greece, Portugal and Spain, of Russia, East Germany, Poland, Hungary, Romania. Think of Argentina and South Africa and other places where change looked hopeless and then it happened. Remember Somoza in Nicaragua scurrying to his private plane, Ferdinand and Imelda Marcos hurriedly assembling their jewels and clothes, the shah of Iran desperately searching for a country that would take him in as he fled the crowds in Tehran, Duvalier in Haiti barely managing to put on his pants to escape the wrath of the Haitian people.

We can't expect George Bush to scurry off in a helicopter. But we can hold him accountable for catapulting the nation into two wars, for the death and dismemberment of tens of thousands of human beings in this country, Afghanistan, and Iraq, and for his violations of the U.S. Constitution and international law. Surely these acts meet the constitutional requirement of "high crimes and misdemeanors" for impeachment.

Indeed, people around the country have begun to call for his impeachment. Of course we cannot expect a craven Congress to impeach him. Congress was willing to impeach Nixon for breaking into a building, but will not impeach Bush for breaking into a country. They were willing to impeach Clinton because of his sexual shenanigans, but will not impeach Bush for turning the wealth of the country over to the superrich.

There has been a worm eating at the innards of the Bush administration's complacency all along: the knowledge of the American public—buried, but in a very shallow grave, easy to disinter—that this government came to power not by popular will but by a political coup. So we may be seeing the gradual disintegration of the legitimacy of this administration, despite its outward confidence.

There is a long history of imperial powers gloating over victories, becoming overextended and overconfident, and not realizing that power is not simply a matter of arms and money. Military power has its limits—limits created by human beings, their sense of justice, and capacity to resist. The United States with 10,000 nuclear weapons could not win in Korea or Vietnam, could not stop a revolution in Cuba or Nicaragua. Likewise, the Soviet Union with its nuclear weapons and huge army was forced to retreat from Afghanistan and could not stop the Solidarity movement in Poland.

A country with military power can destroy but it cannot build. Its citizens become uneasy because their fundamental day-to-day needs are sacrificed for military glory while their young are neglected and sent to war. The uneasiness grows and grows and the citizenry gathers in resistance in larger and larger numbers, which become too many to control; one day the top-heavy empire collapses.

Change in public consciousness starts with low-level discontent, at first vague, with no connection being made between the discontent and the policies of the government. And then the dots begin to connect, indignation increases, and people begin to speak out, organize, and act.

Today, all over the county there is growing awareness of the shortage of teachers, nurses, medical care, and affordable housing, as budget cuts take place in every state of the union. A teacher recently wrote a letter to the *Boston Globe*: "I may be one of 600 Boston teachers who will be laid off as a result of budget shortfalls." The writer then connects it to the billions spent for bombs, for, as he puts it, "sending innocent Iraqi children to hospitals in Baghdad."

There are millions of people in this country opposed to the current war. When you see a statistic "40 percent of Americans support the war," that means that 60 percent of Americans do not. I am convinced that the number of people opposed to the war will continue to rise while the number of war supporters will continue to sink. Along the way, artists, musicians, writers, and cultural workers lend a special emotional and spiritual power to the movement for peace and justice. Rebellion often starts as something cultural.

The challenge remains. On the other side are formidable forces: money, political power, the major media. On our side are the people of the world and a power greater than money or weapons: the truth.

Truth has a power of its own. Art has a power of its own. That age-old lesson—that everything we do matters—is the meaning of the people's struggle here in the United States and everywhere. A poem can inspire a movement. A pamphlet can spark a revolution. Civil disobedience can arouse people and provoke us to think. When we organize with one another, when we get involved, when we stand up and speak out together, we can create a power no government can suppress.

We live in a beautiful country. But people who have no respect for human life, freedom, or justice have taken it over. It is now up to all of us to take it back.

2

THE ULTIMATE BETRAYAL

For months I could not get out of my mind a photograph that appeared on the front page of the *New York Times* on December 30, 2003, alongside a story by Jeffrey Gettleman. It showed a young man sitting on a chair facing a class of sixth graders in Blairsville, Pennsylvania. A woman sat next to him—not the teacher of the class, but the young fellow's mother. She was there to help him because he is blind.

That was Jeremy Feldbusch, then twenty-four years old, a sergeant in the Army Rangers, who was guarding a dam along the Euphrates River on April 3, 2003, when a shell exploded 100 feet away and shrapnel tore into his face. When he came out of a coma in an Army Medical Center five weeks later, he could not see. Two weeks later, he was awarded a Purple Heart and a Bronze Star, but he still could not see. His father, sitting at his bedside, said: "Maybe God thought you had seen enough killing."

Newspapers sometimes report the statistics of how many American GIs have been killed in the Iraq War—477 as of December 30, 2003, more than five times that today—but what is not usually reported is that for every death there are four or five men and women seriously wounded.

The term "seriously wounded" does not begin to convey the horror. Sergeant Feldbusch's mother, Charlene Feldbusch, who, along with his father, virtually lived at his bedside for

17

two months, one day saw a young woman soldier crawling past her in the corridor. She had no legs, and her three-year-old son was trailing behind.

She started to cry. Later she told Gettleman, "Do you know how many times I walked up and down those hallways and saw those people without arms or legs and thought: Why couldn't this be my son? Why his eyes?"

The U.S. government was eager to send young men and women half a world away into the heart of another nation. And even though they have fearsome weapons, they are still vulnerable to guerrilla attacks that are leaving so many of them blinded, crippled, or dead. Is this not the ultimate betrayal of our young by our government?

Their families very often understand this before their sons and daughters do, and remonstrate with them before they go off. Ruth Aitken did so with her son, a U.S. Army captain, telling him it was a war for oil while he insisted he was protecting the country from terrorists. He was killed on April 4, 2003, in a battle around Baghdad airport. "He was doing his job," his mother said. "But it makes me mad that this whole war was sold to the American public and to the soldiers as something it wasn't."

One father, in Escondido, California, Fernando Suarez del Solar, told reporters that his son, a lance corporal in the U.S. Marines, had died for "Bush's oil." Another father in Baltimore, whose son, Kendall Waters-Bey, a staff sergeant in the Marine Corps, was killed, held up a photo of his son for the news cameras and said: "President Bush, you took my only son away from me."

Of course, they and their families are not the only ones being betrayed. The Iraqi people, promised freedom from tyranny, saw their country, already devastated by two wars and twelve years of sanctions, attacked by the most power-ful military machine in history. The Pentagon proudly announced a campaign of "shock and awe," which has left tens of thousands Iraqi men, women, and children dead, and many thousands more maimed.

The list of betrayals is long. The U.S. government has betrayed the hopes of the world for peace. After 50 million died in the Second World War, the United Nations was set up, as its charter promised, "to save succeeding generations from the scourge of war."

The people of the United States have been betrayed, because, with the Cold War over and "the threat of commu-nism" no longer able to justify the stealing of trillions of the public's tax dollars for the military budget, the theft of the national wealth continues. It continues at the expense of children, the elderly, the homeless, the unemployed, and the sick, wiping out the expectations after the fall of the Soviet Union that there would be a "peace dividend" to bring prosperity to all.

And yes, we come back to the ultimate betrayal, the betrayal of the young, sent to war with grandiose promises and lying words about freedom and democracy, duty and patriotism. We are not historically literate enough to remember that these promises—lies—started far back in the country's past.

Young men—boys, in fact—were enticed to join the Revolutionary Army of the Founding Fathers by the grand words of the Declaration of Independence. But they found themselves mistreated, in rags and without boots while their officers lived in luxury and merchants profited from the war. Thousands mutinied, and some were executed by order of General George Washington.

It is a long story, the betrayal of the very ones sent to kill and die in wars. When soldiers realize this, they rebel. In the Civil War there was deep resentment that the rich could buy their way out of service, and that financiers like J. P. Morgan were profiting as the bodies piled up on the battlefields. The black soldiers who joined the Union army and were decisive in the victory came home to poverty and racism.

Soldiers returning from World War I, many of them crippled and shell-shocked, were hit hard, barely a dozen years after the end of the war, by the Depression. Unemployed, their families hungry, they descended on Washington—20,000 of them, from every part of the country. They set up tents across the Potomac from the Capitol and demanded that Congress pay the bonuses it had promised. Instead, the army was called out, and the veterans were fired on, teargassed, and dispersed.

Perhaps it was to wipe out that ugly memory, or perhaps it was the glow accompanying the great victory over fascism, but the veterans of World War II received a GI Bill of Rights—free college education, low-interest home mortgages, life insurance.

The Vietnam War veterans, on the other hand, came home to find that the same government that had sent them into an immoral and fruitless war, leaving many of them wounded in body and mind, now wanted to forget about them.

The United States had sprayed huge parts of Vietnam with the highly toxic chemical defoliant Agent Orange, resulting in hundreds of thousands of Vietnamese deaths, lingering cancers, and birth defects. American GIs were also exposed in great numbers, and tens of thousands, pointing to sickness, to birth defects in their children, asked the

Veterans Administration for help. But the government denied responsibility. However, a suit against Dow Chemical and other manufacturers of the defoliant was settled out of court for $180 million. The case was brought by 15,000 veterans and their relatives.

Today, as the government pours hundreds of billions of dollars into war, it has no money to take care of the Vietnam veterans who are homeless, who linger in VA hospitals, who suffer from mental disorders, and who commit suicide in shocking numbers. It is a bitter legacy.

The United States government was proud that, although perhaps 100,000 Iraqis were killed in the 1990–91 First Gulf War, there were only 148 American battle casualties. What it has concealed from the public is that 206,000 veterans of that war have filed claims with the Veterans Administration (VA) for injuries and illnesses. Since the war, 8,300 veterans have died, and 160,000 claims for disability have been recognized by the VA.

The betrayal of GIs and veterans continues in the so-called war on terror. U.S. soldiers are being killed almost every day in deadly guerrilla warfare that continues to intensify. An article in the *Christian Science Monitor* quotes an officer in the Third Infantry Division in Iraq as saying: "Make no mistake, the level of morale for most soldiers that I've seen has hit rock bottom."

And those who come back alive, but blind or without arms or legs, find that the Bush administration is cutting funds for veterans. Bush's second State of the Union address, while going through the usual motions of thanking those serving in Iraq, continued his policy of ignoring the thousands who have come back wounded, in a war that is becoming increasingly unpopular.

Bush's quick Thanksgiving visit to Iraq in 2003, much ballyhooed in the press, was seen differently by an army nurse in Landstuhl, Germany, where casualties from the war are treated. She sent out an e-mail that read: "My 'Bush Thanksgiving' was a little different. I spent it at the hospital taking care of a young West Point lieutenant wounded in Iraq. . . . When he pressed his fists into his eyes and rocked his head back and forth he looked like a little boy. They all do, all nineteen in the ward that day, some missing limbs, eyes, or worse. . . . It's too bad Bush didn't add us to his holiday agenda. The men said the same, but you'll never read that in the paper."

Throughout both terms of his presidency, George Bush has insisted that our violence in Afghanistan and Iraq has been in the interest of freedom and democracy, and essential to the war on terror. Approximately 75 percent of Americans supported the war on Iraq when it first began. Today, public opinion polls show that less than half of the citizenry support either the president or the war. Despite the reluctance of the major media to show the horrific toll of the war on Iraqi men, women, children, or to show U.S. soldiers with amputated limbs, enough of those images have broken through, coupled with the grimly rising death toll, to have an effect.

But, beyond the hard-core minority who will not be dissuaded by any facts (and it would be a waste of energy to make them the object of our attention), there is still a large pool of Americans who are open to change. For them, it would be important to measure Bush's grandiose rhetoric about the "spread of liberty" against the historical record of American expansion.

It is a challenge not just for teachers to give the young

information they will not get in the standard textbooks, but for everyone else who has an opportunity to speak to friends and neighbors and work associates, to write letters to newspapers, to call in to talk shows.

The history is powerful. Truths make their way, against all obstacles, and break down the credibility of the war makers, juxtaposing what reality teaches against the rhetoric of inaugural addresses and White House briefings. It is our civic responsibility as Americans to enhance that learning, to make clear the disconnect between the rhetoric of "liberty" and the photo of a bloodied little girl, weeping.

It is also our responsibility to go beyond the depiction of past and present and suggest alternatives to the paths of greed and violence. All through history, people working for change have been inspired by visions of a different world. Here in the United States it is possible to point to our enormous national wealth and suggest how, if not wasted on war or siphoned off to the superrich, that wealth can help make possible a truly just society.

The juxtapositions wait to be made. Recent disasters in Asia, alongside the millions dying of AIDS in Africa, cry out for justice in the face of the $500 billion U.S. miltary budget. The words of people from all over the world who gather year after year in Pôrto Alegre, Brazil, and other places—that "another world is possible"—point to a time when national boundaries are erased, when the natural riches of the world are used for everyone. The false promises of the rich and powerful about "spreading liberty" can be fulfilled, not by them, but by the concerted effort of us all, as the truth comes out, and our numbers grow.

As for Jeremy Feldbusch, blinded in the war, his hometown of Blairsville, an old coal-mining town of 3,600, held a parade for him, and the mayor honored him. I thought of the blinded, armless, legless soldier in Dalton Trumbo's novel *Johnny Got His Gun*, who, lying on his hospital cot, unable to speak or hear, remembers when his hometown gave him a send-off, with speeches about fighting for liberty and democracy. He finally learns how to communicate by tapping Morse code letters with his head, and asks the authorities to take him to schoolrooms everywhere, to show the children what war is like. But they do not respond. "In one terrible moment he saw the whole thing," Trumbo writes. "They wanted only to forget him." In a sense, the novel was asking—and now our returning veterans are asking—that we do not forget.

3

SEATTLE: A FLASH OF THE POSSIBLE

I n the year 1919, when the city of Seattle was brought to a halt by a general strike—beginning with 35,000 ship-yard workers demanding a wage increase—the mayor reflected on its significance:

> True there were no flashing guns, no bombs, no killings. Revolution . . . doesn't need violence. The general strike, as practiced in Seattle, is of itself the weapon of revolution, all the more dangerous because quiet. To succeed, it must suspend every-thing, stop the entire life stream of a commu-nity. . . . That is to say, it puts the government out of operation. And that is all there is to revolt—no matter how achieved.

What happened in Seattle in November 1999 was not as large an event as the general strike of 1919. But it showed how apparently powerless people—when united in large numbers—can stop the machinery of government and big business. In an era when the power of government and multinational corporations is overwhelming, it is instruc-tive to get even a hint of how fragile that power is when con-fronted by organized, determined citizens.

When in the early 1960s civil rights activists of the South

put into practice the principle they called "Nonviolent Direct Action," they were able to make heretofore invincible power yield. What happened in Seattle was another manifestation of that principle.

Nonviolent action is not utopian; it is practical as well as moral. It builds on what already exists. It starts not with change in government, but with civil society, with the hearts and minds of people, which is where John Adams said the American Revolution was won. The people can bypass the government and tackle social problems themselves, as has been demonstrated by Havel in Czechoslovakia, Solidarity in Poland, and the indigenous in Chiapas, Mexico.

The strike, the boycott, the refusal to serve, the ability to paralyze the functioning of a complex social structure— these remain potent weapons against the most fearsome state or corporate power.

Note how General Motors and Ford had to surrender to the strikers of the 1930s, how black children marching in Birmingham in 1963 pushed Congress into passing a Civil Rights Act, how the U.S. government, carrying on a war in Vietnam, had to reconsider in the face of draft resistance and desertions en masse, how a garbage workers' strike in New York immobilized a great city, how the threat of a boycott against Texaco for racist policies brought immediate concessions.

The Seattle protests, even if only a gleam of possibility in the disheartening dark of our time, should cause us to recall basic principles of power and powerlessness, so easily forgotten as the flood of media nonsense washes over the history of social movements.

It has been discouraging to watch the control of information in this country get tighter and tighter as megacorporations have taken over television and radio stations, newspapers, even book publishing. And yet, we saw in Seattle that when tens of thousands of men and women fill the streets, halt the normal flow of business, and march with colorful banners, giant puppets, and an infectious enthusiasm, they can break through the barriers of the corporate media and excite the attention of people all over the country and around the world. It is important to remember that the country's first Independent Media Center emerged in Seattle to bypass corporate media and create a source of immediate information on the demonstrations. That single center has since mushroomed into a worldwide network with centers from Chicago to Croatia, Barcelona to Bolivia.

Of course, the television cameras rushed to cover the fires in Seattle (many actually produced by the police with their exploding tear-gas bombs) and the broken windows. The term "anarchist" was used to describe the perpetrators by journalists ignorant of the philosophy of anarchism, as were the window smashers themselves. But it was not lost on viewers that the vast majority of people marching through the streets were angry, even obstructive, but peaceful—yes, *nonviolent direct action.*

In Seattle, the demonstrators were grappling with seemingly impossibly complex economic issues—globalization, protectionism, export trade, intellectual properties, indigenous rights—issues the most sophisticated experts have had a hard time explaining. But through all of that complexity, a certain diamond-hard idea shone through: the schemes of the well-dressed people of finance and government gathering in ornate halls were dangerous to the health and lives of working people all over the world. Thousands in the streets, representing millions, showed their determination to resist these schemes.

In one crucial way, it was a turning point in the history of movements of recent decades—a departure from the single-issue focus of the Seabrook occupation of 1977, the nuclear-freeze rally in Central Park in 1982, and the gatherings in Washington for the Equal Rights Amendment in 1978, for lesbian and gay rights in 1993, for the Million Man March in 1995, and for the Stand for Children in 1996. This time, the union movement was at the center. The issue of class—rich and poor, here and all over the globe—bound everyone together.

It was, at the least, a flash of the possible. It recalled the prophecy of A. Philip Randolph in November of 1963, speaking to an AFL-CIO convention shortly after the Civil Rights March brought 200,000 people, black and white, to the nation's capital. Randolph told the delegates: "The Negro's protest today is but the first rumbling of the under-class. As the Negro has taken to the streets, so will the unemployed of all races take to the streets."

As the people took to the streets in Seattle, so did they later in Washington, Québec, Genoa, Cancún. There will be more rumblings to come.

4

BIG GOVERNMENT

I have seen some of my most stalwart friends flinch before the accusation that they—in asking, let us say, for a single-payer health-care system—call for "big government." So insistent has been the press and both parties of political leadership of the country that "big government" is a plague to be avoided, that otherwise courageous people have retreated before the attack.

It's an issue, therefore, that deserves some examination.

When Bill Clinton, in his 1996 campaign, announced happily that "the era of big government is over," he was suggesting that the United States had gone through an unfortunate phase that had ended.

He was repeating the myth that there once was a golden past where the "free market" reigned and the nation followed Jefferson's idea, which Tom Paine had expressed as: "that government is best which governs least." Big government has been with the world for at least 500 years, and has become very big in this century. Jefferson never followed his own expressed belief, as he doubled U.S. territory with the Louisiana Purchase.

It was the rise of the modern nation-state in the seventeenth century that created big government in order to centralize the tax system and thus raise enough money to subsidize the new worldwide trading organizations like the

Dutch East India Company and the British East India Company. Both of these companies were granted government charters about 1600, giving them monopoly rights to maraud around the world, trading goods and human beings, bringing wealth back to the home country.

The new nation-states had to raise armies and navies to protect the shipping trade, especially the slave trade. They also needed forces to invade other parts of the world and forcibly take land from indigenous people for trading and settling. The state would use its power to drive out foreign competitors and to put down rebellions at home and abroad. "Big government" was needed for the benefit of the mercantile and landowning classes.

Adam Smith, considered the apostle of the "free market," understood very well how capitalism could not survive a truly free market if government was not big enough to protect it. In the middle of the eighteenth century he wrote: "Laws and governments may be considered in this and indeed in every case, a combination of the rich to oppress the poor, and preserve to themselves the inequality of the goods, which would otherwise be soon destroyed by the attacks of the poor, who if not hindered by the government would soon reduce the others to an equality with themselves by open violence."

After the Revolutionary War, class resentment erupted in western Massachusetts, where farmers, many of them veterans of the Revolutionary War, rebelled in 1786 against high taxes ("rates"), foreclosures, and loss of their land and livestock. This was known as Shays' Rebellion after Captain Daniel Shays, the war veteran who led the insurrection.

Shays' Rebellion was suppressed by force, but the conflict between rich and poor was to continue in the early decades of the new Republic, as citizens demanded the democracy that had been promised them in the Declaration.

The American colonists, having fought and won the war for independence from England, faced the question of what kind of government to establish. In 1786 General Henry Knox warned his former commander, George Washington, about rebels: "They see the weakness of government; they feel at once their own poverty, compared to the opulent, and their own force, and they are determined to make use of the latter in order to remedy the former. Their creed is that the property of the U.S. has been protected from the confiscations of Britain by the joint exertions of all, and therefore should be the common property of all."

The Constitutional Convention in Philadelphia for 1787 was called to deal with this problem, to set up "big government," to protect the interests of merchants, slaveholders, and land speculators, to establish law and order, and to avert future rebellions like that of Daniel Shays.

When the debate over ratification of the Constitution took place in the various states, *The Federalist Papers* appeared in the New York press to support ratification. "Federalist No. 10," written by James Madison, made clear why a strong central government was needed: to curb the potential demand of a "majority faction" for "an equal division of property, or for any other improper or wicked object."

And so the U.S. Constitution set up big government to be big enough to protect slaveholders against slave rebellion, to catch runaway slaves if they went from one state to another, to pay off bondholders, to pass tariffs on behalf of manufacturers, and to tax poor farmers to pay for armies that would then attack the farmers if they resisted payment, as was done in the Whiskey Rebellion in Pennsylvania in 1794.

Much of this was embodied in the legislation of the first Congress, responding to the request of Alexander Hamilton, the Secretary of the Treasury.

For all of our nation's history, this legislative pattern has been the norm. Government has defended the interests of the wealthy classes. It has raised tariffs higher and higher to help manufacturers, given subsidies to shipping interests, and 100 million acres of free land to the railroads. It has used the armed forces to clear indigenous communities off their land, suppress labor uprisings, and invade countries in the Caribbean for the benefit of American growers, bankers, and investors. This was very big government.

When the Great Depression produced social turmoil, with strikes and protests all over the nation, the government responded with laws for Social Security (which one angry senator said would "take all the romance out of life"), unemployment insurance, subsidized housing, work programs, and money for the arts. In the atmosphere created by the movements of the 1960s, Medicare and Medicaid were enacted. Only then did the cry arise, among politicians and the press, continuing to this day, warning of the evils of "big government."

Of course, alarm about "big government" has not extended to the enormous subsidies given to big business. After World War II, the aircraft industries, which had made enormous profits during the war (92 percent of their expansion paid for by the government), were in decline. Stuart Symington, Assistant Secretary of War for Air, wrote to the president of Aircraft Industries: "It looks as if our airplane industry is in trouble, and it would seem to be the obligation of our little shop to do the best we can to help." The help came and has never stopped coming. Billions in subsidies pour in each year to produce fighter planes and bombers.

When Chrysler ran out of cash in 1980, the government stepped in to help. (Try that the next time you run out of cash.) Tax benefits, like the oil-depletion allowance, added up over the years to hundreds of billions of dollars. The *New York Times* reported in 1984 that the twelve top military contractors paid an average tax rate of 1.5 percent while middle-class Americans were paying 15 percent and more.

So it's time to gently point out the hypocrisy when you hear both Democrats and Republicans decry "big government." With only a bit of reflection, it becomes clear that the issue is not big or little government, but *government for whom*? Is it the ideal expressed by Lincoln—government "for the people"—or is it the reality described by the Populist orator Mary Elizabeth Lease in 1890—"a government of Wall Street, by Wall Street, and for Wall Street"?

There is good evidence that the American people, whose common sense often resists the most virulent propaganda campaigns, understand this. Political leaders and the press have pounded away at their sensibilities with fearful talk of "big government," and so long as it remains an abstraction, it is easy for people to go along, each listener defining it in his or her own way. But when specific questions are asked, the results are illuminating.

Again and again, public opinion surveys over the last decade have shown that people want the government to act to remedy economic injustice. At one point the Pew Research Center asked "[is it] the responsibility of the government to take care of people who can't take care of themselves?" and 61 percent said they either completely agreed or mostly agreed. When, after the Republican congressional

victory in 1994 the *New York Times* asked people their opin-
ions on "welfare," the responses were evenly for and against.
The *Times* headline read: "Public Shows Trust in GOP
Congress," but this misled its readers, because when the
question was posed more specifically: "Should the government help people in need?" more than 65 percent answered
affirmatively.

This should not surprise us. The achievements of the
New Deal programs still glow warmly in the public memory:
Social Security, unemployment insurance, the public works
programs, the minimum wage, the subsidies for the arts.
There is an initial worried reaction when people are con-
fronted with the scare words "big government." But that falls
away as soon as someone points to the GI Bill of Rights,
Medicare, Medicaid, food stamps, and loans to small business.

So let's not hesitate to say: We want the government,
responding to the Lincolnian definition of democracy, to
organize a system that gives free medical care to everyone
and pays for it out of a reformed tax system that is truly progressive. In short, we want everyone to be in the position
of U.S. senators and members of the armed forces—bene-
ficiaries of big, benevolent government.

"Big government" in itself is hardly the issue. The question is: Whom will it serve? Or rather, which class?

5

THE FORBIDDEN WORD: CLASS

P olitical leaders often become annoyed when someone suggests that we live in a class society dominated by moneyed interests. During recent presidential campaigns, Republicans and Democrats have battled their way to the White House without ever acknowledging that a wide range of economic classes exist in this country. Only Ralph Nader dared to suggest that the United States is divided among the rich, the poor, and the nervous in between. Such talk is considered politically intolerable and was enough to have Nader barred from the nationally televised presidential debates.

The U.S. political establishment insists that we mustn't talk about class. Only Marxists do that, although thirty years before Marx was born, James Madison, "Father of the Constitution," said that there was an inevitable conflict in society between those who had property and those who did not.

Our political leaders would prefer us to believe we are one family—me and Exxon, you and Microsoft, the children of the CEOs and the children of the restaurant workers. We must believe our interests are the same. That's why officials speak of going to war "for the national interest," as if it were in *all* our interest.

That's also why we maintain an enormous military budget for "national security," as if our nuclear weapons strengthen the security of all and not the securities of some. It's also why our culture is soaked in a particular strain of patriotism, the idea of which is piped into our consciousness from first grade onward when we begin every schoolday by reciting the Pledge of Allegiance to the Flag: "one nation, under God, indivisible, with liberty and justice for all."

I remember stumbling over that big word "indivisible" at the age of six. Only later did I begin to understand that our nation, from the start, has been divided by class, race, national origin, and has been beset by fierce conflicts—yes, class conflicts—throughout all our history.

Mainstream culture labors strenuously to keep that out of the history books, to maintain the idea of a monolithic, noble "us" against a shadowy but unmistakably evil "them." It starts with the story of the American Revolution, and, as the movie *The Patriot* (kindergarten history, put on screen for millions of viewers) tells us once more, we were united in glorious struggle against British rule. The mythology surrounding the Founding Fathers is based on the idea that we Americans are indeed one family and that our Constitution represents all our interests, as declared proudly by the opening words of its preamble: "We, the people of the United States."

It may therefore seem surly for us to acknowledge that the American Revolution was not a war waged by a united population. The 150 years leading up to the Revolution were filled with class conflict. Thus, when the Revolutionary War began, some colonists saw the war as one of liberation, but many others saw it as the substitution of one set of rulers for another. As for enslaved black people and American Indians, there was little to choose between the British and the Americans.

The nation came into existence with the stirring language

of the Declaration of Independence, a manifesto of democracy. It promised an equal right to "Life, Liberty, and the pursuit of Happiness." However, those noble words concealed harsh realities about the American colonies that rebelled against England. They obviously did not apply to the enslaved black people who made up almost 20 percent of the colonial population; indeed, Jefferson was rebuffed when he attempted to introduce a paragraph in the Declaration denouncing the slave trade. The words of the Declaration also did not apply to indigenous Americans, who were described as "merciless Indian Savages."

The Declaration of Independence, pretending to national unity against British rule, gave little indication that the Revolutionaries were not united in their enthusiasm for independence, that American society had long been riven by internal conflicts—servants and slaves against their masters, tenants against landlords, poor people in the cities rioting for food and flour against profiteering merchants, mutinies of sailors against their captains.

There was not unswerving enthusiasm within the Revolutionary Army that fought for independence from England. The historian Eric Foner describes the war as "a time of immense profits for some colonists and terrible hardships for others." The class differences were keenly felt in the ranks of the army, where "terrible hardships" fell, not upon the officer class, who were well-fed, well-clothed, well-paid, but upon the rank-and-file soldier.

In October of 1779, with the war four years old, the city of Philadelphia witnessed what came to be known as the "Fort Wilson riot." Soldiers marched into the city and to the house of James Wilson, a wealthy lawyer, protesting what they considered profiteering from the war and

Wilson's opposition to the democratic constitution adopted in Pennsylvania.

During the Revolution, casualties exceeded, in proportion to population, American casualties in World War II. Inside the Revolution, class conflict came dramatically alive with mutinies from George Washington's army. In 1781, after enduring five years of war, more than one thousand soldiers from Pennsylvania—mostly foreign born, from Ireland, Scotland, Germany—dispersed their officers, killing a captain, wounding others, and marched, armed with cannon, toward the Continental Congress at Philadelphia. They had seen their officers paid handsomely, fed and clothed well, while the privates and sergeants were fed slop, marched in rags without shoes, were paid in virtually worthless Continental currency, or were not paid at all for months. They were abused, beaten, and whipped by their officers for the smallest breach of discipline. Their deepest grievance was that they wanted out of the war, claiming their terms of enlistment had expired, and they were kept in the army by force. (Today, a similar grievance is felt by the many U.S. soldiers in Iraq who are forced by the U.S. government to stay beyond their terms of duty, a policy the military euphemistically calls "Stop Loss.") They were aware that in the spring of 1780 eleven Morristown deserters were sentenced to death but at the last minute received a reprieve, except for one soldier who had forged discharges for a hundred men. He was hanged.

General Washington, facing by this time 1,700 mutineers—a substantial part of his army—assembled at Princeton, New Jersey, and decided to make concessions. Many of the rebels were allowed to leave the army, and Washington asked the governors of the various states for money to deal with the grievances of the soldiers. The Pennsylvania line quieted down.

But when another mutiny broke out in the New Jersey line, involving only a few hundred, Washington ordered harsh measures. He saw the possibility of "this dangerous spirit" spreading. Two of "the most atrocious offenders" were court-martialed on the spot and sentenced to be shot. Their fellow mutineers, some of them weeping as they did so, carried out the executions.

Howard Fast tells the story of the mutinies in his novel *The Proud and the Free*. Drawing from the classic historical account in Carl Van Doren's *Mutiny in January*, Fast dramatizes the class conflict inside the Revolutionary Army. One of his characters, the mutinous soldier Jack Maloney, recalls the words of Thomas Paine and the promise of freedom and says that, yes, he is willing to die for that freedom, but "not for that craven Congress in Philadelphia, not for the fine Pennsylvania ladies in their silks and satins, not for the property of every dirty lord and fat patroon in New Jersey."

In the Mexican War of 1846–48, an American army marched into Mexico and quickly defeated the opposing force, with the result that the United States took almost half of Mexico's territory. The U.S. Army consisted of volunteers, half of them recent immigrants from Ireland and Germany, lured by money and the promise of a hundred acres of land. But disillusionment grew quickly as the battles became bloody, and sickness, suffering, and death plagued the soldiers. Desertions multiplied, and as General Winfield Scott moved toward the final battle for Mexico City, seven of his eleven regiments evaporated, their enlistment times up. The Massachusetts volunteers—the half who survived the war—booed their commanding officer at a reception after the war ended.

Class anger erupted again during the Civil War in both Northern and Confederate armies. The draft riots in New York and other cities, protesting the fact that the rich could buy their way out of military service, were reflections of this anger. In the South, as the war went on, desertions grew, often stirred by the fact that the families of soldiers back home were going hungry while plantation owners, more concerned with profits than with patriotism, were growing cotton instead of food.

When the War for Independence was won, a new government was formed to serve the interests of slaveholders, merchants, and manufacturers, while offering white males with some property a degree of influence, but not dominance, in the political process.

By its domestic and foreign policies, the new American government would maintain the dominant position of the wealthy in society over the next two centuries and beyond. Its legislation would be class legislation, tariffs for the manufacturers, subsidies for the railroads, oil companies, and other giant corporations. Armed force would be used to expel the American Indian tribes from their land, open the West to enterprise, and put down rebellious workers who went out on strike.

The history of the 200 years that followed the Revolution is a history of control of the nation by one class, as the government, solidly in the hands of the rich, gave huge gifts of the nation's resources to the railroad magnates, the industrialists, and the shipowners. Historian Charles Beard, in the first years of the Great Depression, wrote caustically about "The Myth of Rugged American Individualism," noting that industrial and financial leaders were not rugged enough to make their own way in the world and had to be subsidized, and silver-spoon-fed, by the government.

Pointing to class divisions in this country has always been dangerous. Thus, when Eugene V. Debs, opposing World War I, told an assembly in Ohio that "the master class has always brought a war, and the subject class has always fought the battle," he was not tolerated. Debs was sentenced to ten years in prison. Oliver Wendell Holmes, in the spirit of patriotic liberalism, affirmed the sentence for a unanimous Supreme Court.

Today, even the slightest suggestion that we are a nation divided by class brings angry reactions. However, reality repeatedly exposes the myth of a classless society, as when Hurricane Katrina devastated New Orleans, and the whole world could see how the desperation of the poor and the black was ignored by the government.

The fact that half the population does not vote is itself a sign that the poor, who make up most of the nonvoters, do not feel represented by either of the major parties. A *New York Times* reporter, in a rare excursion into "the other America," spoke to people in Cross City, Florida, during a recent presidential election and concluded: "People here look at [the two opposing candidates] and see two men born to the country club, men whose family histories jingle with silver spoons. They appear, to people here, just the same."

Cindy Lamb, a cashier at a Chevron filling station, and wife of a construction worker, told the reporter: "I don't think they think about people like us, and if they do care, they're not going to do anything for us. Maybe if they had ever lived in a two bedroom trailer, it would be different."

An African American woman, a manager at McDonald's

who makes slightly more than the minimum wage, said about the two opposing presidential candidates: "I don't even pay attention to those two, and all my friends say the same. My life won't change."

In other nations, class difference is not so obscured. During the 2006 presidential campaign in Mexico, the Mexican people had a choice between a range of candidates who represented clearly different class interests and who spoke publicly about those differences. Not so here. Come the next U.S. presidential election, we can expect the same class that has always dominated our political and economic systems to continue to control the issues discussed, continue to exclude candidates like Ralph Nader from national debate, and, thus, continue to hold power. Citizens will therefore face the same challenge the day after the election that we have always faced: how to bring together the class of have-nots—a great majority of the country—into the kind of social movement that in the past has gained some measure of justice and has made the people in charge tremble at the prospect of "class warfare."

Since it imposes silence on these issues, our political system—bipartisan in its coldness to human rights—cannot be respected. It can only be protested against, challenged, or, in the words of the Declaration of Independence, referring to a government that has violated its responsibility to its people, be "altered or abolished." That's a tall order, but we can prepare for it by a multitude of short steps in which citizens and immigrants organize social movements outside of the party system.

Such movements, responding to the great challenges of the new century, can transform the current system and bring us closer to real democracy.

6

WORLD WAR II:
THE GOOD WAR

The notion of the "good war" comes up often when I speak in public. When I was invited by the Smithsonian Institution to participate in a Memorial Day celebration panel, the idea came up again. The person who called to invite me said that the theme would be "War Stories." I told him that I would come, not to tell "war stories," but rather to talk about World War II and its meaning for us today. Fine, he said.

I made my way into a scene that looked like a movie set for a Cecil B. DeMille extravaganza: huge tents pitched here and there, hawkers with souvenirs, thousands of visitors, many of them clearly World War II veterans, some in old uniforms, sporting military caps and wearing their medals. In the tent designated for my panel, I joined my fellow panelist, an African American woman who had served with the Women's Army Corps in World War II and who would speak about her personal experiences in a racially segregated army.

I was introduced as a veteran of the Army Air Corps, a bombardier who had flown combat missions over Europe in the last months of the war. I wasn't sure how this audience would react to what I had to say about the war, in that atmosphere of celebration, in the honoring of the dead, in the glow of a great victory accompanied by countless acts of military heroism.

43

This, roughly, is what I said: "I'm here to honor the two guys who were my closest buddies in the Air Corps—Joe Perry and Ed Plotkin, both of whom were killed in the last weeks of the war. And to honor all the others who died in that war. But I'm not here to honor war itself. I'm not here to honor the men in Washington who send the young to war. I'm certainly not here to honor those in authority who are now waging an immoral war in Iraq."

I went on: "World War II was not simply and purely a 'good war.' It was accompanied by too many atrocities on our side—too many bombings of civilian populations. There were too many betrayals of the principles for which the war was supposed to have been fought.

"Yes, World War II had a strong moral aspect to it—the defeat of fascism. But I deeply resent the way the so-called good war has been used to cast its glow over all the immoral wars we have fought in the past fifty years: in Vietnam, Laos, Cambodia, Grenada, Panama, Iraq, Afghanistan. I certainly don't want our government to use the triumphal excitement surrounding World War II to cover up the horrors now taking place in Iraq.

"I don't want to honor military heroism; that conceals too much death and suffering. I want to honor those who all these years have opposed the horror of war."

The audience applauded. But I wasn't sure what that meant. I knew I was going against the grain of orthodoxy, the romanticization of the war in movies and television, and the war memorial celebrations in the nation's capital.

There was a question-and-answer period. The first person to walk up front was a veteran of World War II, wearing parts of his old uniform. He spoke into the microphone: "I was wounded in World War II and have a Purple Heart to show for it. If President Bush were here right now I would throw that medal in his face."

There was a moment of what I think was shock at the force of his statement. Then applause. I wondered if I was witnessing a phenomenon that recurs often in society: when one voice speaks out against the conventional wisdom and is recognized as speaking truth, people are drawn out of their previous silence.

I was encouraged by the thought that it is possible to challenge the standard glorification of the Second World War, and more important, to refuse to allow it to give war a good name. I did not want this celebration to make it easy for the American public to accept whatever monstrous adventure is cooked up by the establishment in Washington.

More and more, I am finding that I am not the only veteran of World War II who refuses to be corralled into justifying the wars of today, drawing on the emotional and moral capital of World War II. There are other veterans who do not want to overlook the moral complexity of World War II: the imperial intentions of the Allies even as they declared it a war against fascism and for democracy; the deliberate bombing of civilian populations to destroy the morale of the enemy.

Paul Fussell was an infantry lieutenant who was badly wounded while a platoon leader in France in World War II.

"For the past fifty years the Allied war has been sanitized and romanticized almost beyond recognition by the sentimental, the loony patriotic, the ignorant, and the bloodthirsty," he wrote in *Wartime: Understanding and Behavior in the Second World War*.

It was easier, after the end of World War II, to point to the war's stupidities and cruelties in fiction rather than through more direct methods. Thus, Joseph Heller in *Catch-22* captured the idiocy of military life, the crass profiteering, the pointless bombings. And Kurt Vonnegut, in *Slaughterhouse-Five*, brought to a large readership the awful story of the bombing of Dresden.

My own delayed criticism of the war—I had volunteered and was an enthusiastic bombardier—began with reflecting about my participation in the bombing of Royan. This was a small town on the Atlantic coast of France, where several thousand German soldiers had been overrun and were waiting for the war to end. Twelve hundred heavy bombers flew over the vicinity of Royan and dropped napalm, killing German soldiers and French civilians, destroying what was once a beautiful little resort town.

Recently, a man wrote to me who had heard me speak on the radio about that bombing mission and said he was also on that mission. After the war, he became a fireman, then a carpenter, and is now a strong opponent of war. He told me of a friend of his who was also on that mission and who has been arrested many times in antiwar actions. I was encouraged to hear that.

World War II veterans get in touch with me from time to time. One is Edward Wood Jr. of Denver, who upon hearing that I was going to be at the Washington Memorial, wrote to me. He said, "If I were there, I would say: As a combat veteran of World War II, severely wounded in France in 1944, never the man I might have been because of that wound, I so wish that this memorial to World War II might have been made of more than stone or marble. I mourn my generation's failures since its victory in World War II . . . our legacy of incessant warfare in smaller nations far from our borders."

Another airman, Ken Norwood, was shot down on his tenth mission over Europe and spent a year as a prisoner of war in Germany. He has written a memoir (unpublished, so far) that he says is "intentionally an antiwar war story." Packed first into a boxcar, and then forced to march for two weeks through Bavaria in the spring of 1945, Norwood saw the mangled corpses of the victims of Allied bombs, the working-class neighborhoods destroyed. All his experiences, he says, "add to the harsh testimony about the futility and obscenity of war."

The glorification of the "good war" persists in television and film, in the press, and in the pretentious speeches by politicians. The more ugly the stories that come out of Iraq—the bombing of civilians, the mutilation of children, the invasion of homes, and now the torture of prisoners— the more urgent it is for our government to try to crowd out all those images with the triumphant stories of D-Day and World War II.

Those who fought in that war are perhaps better able than anyone else to insist that whatever moral standing can be attached to that war must not be used to turn our eyes away from U.S. atrocities in Afghanistan, Iraq, and around the world.

7

LEARNING FROM HIROSHIMA

Near the end of the novel *The English Patient* there is a passage in which Kip, the Sikh defuser of mines, begins to speak bitterly to the burned, near-death patient about British and American imperialism: "You and then the Americans converted us. . . . You had wars like cricket. How did you fool us into this? Here, listen to what you people have done." He puts earphones on the blackened head. The radio is telling about the bombs dropped on Hiroshima and Nagasaki.

Kip goes on: "All those speeches of civilization from kings and queens and presidents . . . such voices of abstract order . . . American, French, I don't care. When you start bombing the brown races of the world, you're an Englishman. You had King Leopold of Belgium, and now you have fucking Harry Truman of the USA."

If you saw the film version of *The English Patient*, you probably don't remember those lines. That's because they are not there.

Hardly a surprise. The bombing of Hiroshima remains sacred to the American Establishment and to a very large part of the population in this country. I learned that when, in 1995, I was invited to speak at the Chautauqua Institute in New York State. I chose Hiroshima as my subject, it being the fiftieth anniversary of the United States' dropping the bomb. There were 2,000 people in that huge amphitheater, and as I explained why Hiroshima and Nagasaki were unforgivable atrocities perpetrated on a Japan ready to surrender, the audience was silent. Well, not quite; a number of people angrily shouted at me from their seats.

It's understandable. To question Hiroshima is to threaten a precious myth that we all grow up with in this country. According to the myth, America is different from the other countries of the world; other nations commit unspeakable acts, but we do not.

Further, to see it as a wanton act of gargantuan cruelty rather than as an unavoidable necessity ("to end the war, to save lives") would be to raise disturbing questions about the essential goodness of the "good war."

I recall that in junior high school, a teacher asked our class: "What is the difference between a totalitarian state and a democratic state?" The correct answer: "A totalitarian state, unlike ours, believes in using any means to achieve its end."

That was at the start of World War II, when the fascist states were bombing civilian populations in Ethiopia, Spain, England, and Holland. President Roosevelt called the bombings "inhuman barbarism." That was before the United States and England began to bomb civilian populations in Hamburg, Frankfurt, Dresden, and then in Tokyo, Hiroshima, Nagasaki.

Any means to an end is a totalitarian philosophy, one that is shared by all nations that make war.

What means could be more horrible than the burning, mutilation, blinding, and irradiation of hundreds of thousands of Japanese men, women, and children? And yet it is absolutely essential for our political leaders to defend the bombing because if Americans can be induced to accept that, then they can accept any war, any means, so long as the war makers can supply a reason. And there are always plausible reasons delivered from on high as from Moses on the Mount.

Thus, the 3 million killed in Korea can be justified by North Korean aggression, the millions killed in Southeast Asia can be justified by the threat of communism, the invasion of the Dominican Republic in 1965 can be justified by the need to protect American citizens, the support of death squad governments in Central America can be justified in order to stop communism, the invasion of Grenada can be justified to save American medical students, the invasion of Panama to stop the drug trade, the First Gulf War to liberate Kuwait, and the Yugoslav bombing to stop ethnic cleansing.

There is endless room for more wars, with an endless supply of reasons ready to justify them.

That is why the atomic bombings of Hiroshima and Nagasaki are important, because if citizens can question that, if they can declare nuclear weapons an unacceptable means, even if it ends a war a month or two sooner, they may be led to a larger question—the means (involving 40 million killed) used to defeat fascism.

And if people begin to question the moral purity of "the good war," indeed, the very best of wars, then they may get into a questioning mood that will not stop until war itself is questionable, whatever reasons are advanced.

So now, fifty-plus years later, with those bombings still so sacred that a mildly critical Smithsonian exhibit could not be tolerated, we must continue to insist on questioning those deadly missions of August 6 and 9, 1945.

The principal justification for obliterating Hiroshima and Nagasaki continues to be that it "saved lives," that without the bombings, a planned U.S. invasion of Japan would have been necessary, resulting in the killing of tens of thousands, perhaps hundreds of thousands. Truman at one point used the figure "a half million lives," and Churchill "a million lives," but these were figures pulled out of the air to calm troubled consciences; even official projections for the number of casualties in an invasion did not go beyond 46,000 people.

In fact, the bombs that fell on Hiroshima and Nagasaki did not forestall an invasion of Japan because no invasion was necessary. The Japanese were on the verge of surrender, and American military leaders knew that. General Eisenhower, briefed by Secretary of War Henry Stimson on the imminent use of the bomb, told him that "Japan was already defeated and that dropping the bomb was completely unnecessary."

After the bombing, Admiral William D. Leary, Chairman of the Joint Chiefs of Staff, called the atomic bomb "a barbarous weapon," also noting that: "The Japanese were already defeated and ready to surrender."

The Japanese had begun to move to end the war after the U.S. victory on Okinawa, in May of 1945, in the bloodiest battle of the Pacific War. After the middle of June, six members of the Japanese Supreme War Council authorized Foreign Minister Togo to approach the Soviet Union, which was not at war with Japan, to mediate an end to the war "if possible by September."

Togo sent Ambassador Sato to Moscow to feel out the possibility of a negotiated surrender. On July 13, 1945, four days before, Truman, Churchill, and Stalin met in Potsdam to prepare for the end of the war. Germany had surrendered two months earlier. Togo sent a telegram to Sato: "Unconditional surrender is the only obstacle to peace. It is his Majesty's heart's desire to see the swift termination of the war."

The United States knew about that telegram because the United States had broken the Japanese code early in the war. American officials also knew that the Japanese resistance to unconditional surrender was because they had one condition enormously important to them: the retention of the emperor as symbolic leader. Former Ambassador to Japan Joseph Grew and others who knew something about Japanese society had suggested that allowing Japan to keep its emperor would save countless lives by bringing an early end to the war.

Yet Truman would not relent, and the Potsdam Conference agreed to insist on "unconditional surrender." This ensured that the experimental atom bombs would be detonated over Hiroshima and Nagasaki.

It seems that the United States government was determined to drop those bombs.

But why? Gar Alperovitz, whose research on that question is unmatched (see his book *The Decision to Use the Atomic Bomb*), concluded, based on the papers of Truman, his chief adviser James Byrnes, and others, that the bomb was seen as a diplomatic weapon against the Soviet Union. Byrnes advised Truman that the bomb "could let us dictate the terms of ending the war." The British scientist P. M. S. Blackett, one of Churchill's advisers, wrote after the war that dropping the atomic bomb was "the first major operation of the cold diplomatic war with Russia."

There is also evidence that domestic politics played an important role in the decision. In his recent book, *Freedom from Fear: The American People in Depression and War, 1929-1945*, David Kennedy quotes Secretary of State Cordell Hull advising Byrnes, before the Potsdam Conference, that "terrible political repercussions would follow in the U.S." if the unconditional surrender principle would be abandoned. The president would be "crucified" if he did that, Byrnes said. Kennedy reports that "Byrnes accordingly repudiated the suggestions of Leahy, McCloy, Grew, and Stimson," all of whom were willing to relax the "unconditional surrender" demand just enough to permit the Japanese their face-saving requirement for ending the war.

Can we believe that our political leaders would consign hundreds of thousands of people to death or lifelong suffering because of "political repercussions" at home?

The idea is horrifying, yet we can see in history a pattern of presidential behavior that placed personal ambition high above human life. The tapes of John F. Kennedy reveal him weighing withdrawal from Vietnam against the upcoming election. Transcripts of Lyndon Johnson's White House conversations show him agonizing over Vietnam ("I don't think it's worth fighting for . . .") but deciding that he could not withdraw because: "They'd impeach a President—wouldn't they?" Did millions die in Southeast Asia because American presidents wanted to stay in office?

And was not the Clinton-Gore support for the "Star Wars" antimissile program (against all scientific evidence or common sense) prompted by their desire to be seen by the voters as tough guys?

Of course, political ambition was not the only reason for Hiroshima, Vietnam, and the other horrors of our time. There was tin, rubber, oil, corporate profit, imperial arrogance. There is always a cluster of factors, none of them, despite the claims of our leaders, having to do with human rights or human life.

The wars go on, even when they are over. Every day for years after Gulf War I, British and U.S. warplanes bombed Iraq, and civilians and children died. Children also died every day in Iraq because of the U.S.-sponsored embargo. Then George W. Bush came to the White House and invaded again, with civilians in Iraq now being killed at the rate of more than 3,000 *per month*. Every day, boys and girls in Afghanistan step on land mines and are killed or mutilated. The Russia of "the free market" brutalizes Chechnya, as the Russia of "socialism" sent an army into Afghanistan. In the summer of 2006, Israel shelled neighboring Lebanon for one month.

The mine defuser in *The English Patient* was properly bitter about Western imperialism. But the problem is larger than even the five-hundred-year assault on the world's people of color. It is a problem of the corruption of human intelligence, enabling our leaders to create plausible reasons for monstrous acts, to exhort citizens to accept those reasons, and to train soldiers to follow orders. So long as that continues, we will need to refute those reasons and resist those exhortations.

8

UNSUNG HEROES

A high school student recently confronted me: "I read in your book *A People's History of the United States* about the massacres of Indians, the long history of racism, the persistence of poverty in the richest country in the world, the senseless wars. How can I keep from being thoroughly alienated and depressed?"

It's a question I've heard many times before. Another question often put to me by students is this: "Don't we need our national idols? You are taking down all our national heroes—the Founding Fathers, Andrew Jackson, Abraham Lincoln, Theodore Roosevelt, Woodrow Wilson, John F. Kennedy."

Granted, it is good to have historical figures we can admire and emulate. But why hold up as models the fifty-five rich white men who drafted the Constitution as a way of establishing a government that would protect the interests of their class—slaveholders, merchants, bondholders, land speculators?

Why not recall the humanitarianism of William Penn, an early colonist who made peace with the Delaware Indians instead of warring on them, as other colonial leaders were doing?

Why not John Woolman, who, in the years before the Revolution, refused to pay taxes to support the British wars and who spoke out against slavery?

Why go along with the hero worship, so universal in our history textbooks, of Andrew Jackson, the slave owner and killer of American Indians? Jackson was the architect of the Trail of Tears that resulted in the deaths of 4,000 of 16,000 Cherokees who were kicked off their land in Georgia and sent into exile in Oklahoma.

Why not replace him as national icon with John Ross, a Cherokee chief who resisted the dispossession of his people and whose wife died on the Trail of Tears? Or the Seminole leader Osceola, imprisoned and finally killed for leading a guerrilla campaign against the removal of the American Indians?

And while we're at it, should not the Lincoln Memorial be joined by a memorial to Frederick Douglass, who better represented the struggle against slavery? It was that struggle of black and white abolitionists, growing into a great national movement, that pushed a reluctant Lincoln into finally issuing a half-hearted Emancipation Proclamation, and that persuaded Congress to pass the Thirteenth, Fourteenth, and Fifteenth Amendments.

Take another presidential hero, Theodore Roosevelt, who is always near the top of the tiresome lists of Our Greatest Presidents. There he is on Mount Rushmore, as a permanent reminder of our historical amnesia about his racism, his militarism, his love of war.

Why not replace him—granted, removing him from Mount Rushmore will take some doing—with Mark Twain? Roosevelt, remember, had congratulated the American general who in 1906 ordered the massacre of hundreds of men, women, and children on a Philippine island. As vice president of the Anti-Imperialist League, Twain denounced this and continued to point out the cruelties committed in the

Philippine war under the slogan "My country, right or wrong."

Shouldn't we also remind the admirers of Woodrow Wilson, another honored figure in the pantheon of American liberalism, that he insisted on racial segregation in federal buildings, attacked the Mexican coast, sent an occupation army into Haiti and the Dominican Republic, brought our country into the hell of World War I, and put antiwar protesters in prison?

Should we not bring forward as a national hero Emma Goldman, one of those Wilson sent to prison, or Helen Keller, who fearlessly spoke out against the war?

And enough worship of John F. Kennedy, a Cold Warrior who began the covert war in Indochina, went along with the planned invasion of Cuba, and was slow to act against racial segregation in the South.

Should we not replace the portraits of our presidents, which too often take up all the space on our classroom walls, with the likenesses of grassroots heroes like Fannie Lou Hamer, the Mississippi sharecropper? Mrs. Hamer was evicted from her farm and tortured in prison after she joined the civil rights movement, but she became an eloquent voice for freedom. Should we not also celebrate Ella Baker, whose wise counsel and support guided the young black people in the Student Nonviolent Coordinating Committee, the militant edge of the civil rights movement in the Deep South?

In the year 1992, the quincentennial of Christopher Columbus's arrival in this hemisphere, there were meetings all over the country to celebrate him, but there were also, for the first time, gatherings to challenge the customary exaltation of the Great Discoverer. I was at a symposium in New Jersey where I pointed to the terrible crimes against the indigenous people of Hispaniola committed by Columbus and his fellow Spaniards. Afterward, the other man on the platform—chairman of the New Jersey Columbus Day celebration—said to me: "You don't understand; we Italian Americans need our heroes." Yes, I understood the desire for heroes, I said, but why choose a murderer and kidnapper for such an honor? Why not choose Joe DiMaggio or Toscanini or Fiorello LaGuardia or Sacco and Vanzetti? The man was not persuaded.

The same misguided values that have made slaveholders, Indian killers, and militarists the heroes of our history books still operate today. We have heard Senator John McCain, Republican of Arizona, repeatedly referred to as a war hero. Yes, we must sympathize with McCain's ordeal as a war prisoner in Vietnam, where he endured cruelties. But must we call someone a hero who participated in the invasion of a far-off country and dropped bombs on men, women, and children?

I came across only one voice in the mainstream press daring to dissent from the general admiration for McCain—that of the poet, novelist, and *Boston Globe* columnist James Carroll. Carroll contrasted the heroism of McCain, the warrior, to that of Philip Berrigan, who has gone to prison dozens of times for protesting the war in Vietnam and the dangerous nuclear arsenal maintained by our government. Carroll wrote: "Berrigan, in jail, is the truly free man, while McCain remains imprisoned in an unexamined sense of martial honor."

Our country is full of heroic people who are not presidents or military leaders or Wall Street wizards, but who are doing something to keep alive the spirit of resistance to injustice and war.

I think of Kathy Kelly and all the people from Voices in the Wilderness who, in defiance of federal law, traveled to Iraq more than a dozen times to bring food and medicine to people who were suffering under the U.S.-imposed sanctions. I think of Cindy Sheehan and the women of Code Pink who have now camped outside President Bush's vacation home, in Crawford, Texas, two summers in a row as a way of protesting the U.S. occupation of Iraq.

I think also of the thousands of students on more than one hundred college campuses across the country who have protested their universities' connection with sweatshop-produced apparel.

I think of the four McDonald sisters in Minneapolis, all nuns, who have gone to jail repeatedly for protesting against the Alliant Techsystem's production of land mines.

I think, too, of the thousands of people who have traveled to Fort Benning, Georgia, to demand the closing of the murderous School of the Americas.

I think of the West Coast longshoremen who participated in an eight-hour work stoppage to protest the death sentence levied against Mumia Abu-Jamal.

And so many more.

We all know individuals—most of them unsung, unrecognized—who have, often in the most modest ways, spoken out or acted on their beliefs for a more egalitarian, more just, peace-loving society.

To ward off alienation and gloom, it is only necessary to remember the unremembered heroes of the past and to look around us for the unnoticed heroes of the present.

9

TENNIS ON THE *TITANIC*

During the Gore/Bush/Nader presidential election, while the entire nation was hypnotized by the spectacle, I had a vision. I saw the *Titanic* churning through the waters of the North Atlantic toward an iceberg looming in the distance, while passengers and crew concentrated on a tennis game taking place on deck.

In our election-obsessed culture, everything else going on in the world—war, hunger, official brutality, sickness, the violence of everyday life for huge numbers of people—is swept out of the way while the media covers every volley of the candidates. Thus, the superficial crowds out the meaningful, and this is very useful for those who do not want citizens to look beyond the surface of the system. Hidden by the contest of the candidates are real issues of race, class, war, and peace, which the public is not supposed to think about.

As the presidential match came to its frenzied finish, the media kept referring to the Hayes-Tilden election of 1876. The education the public received about this was typical of what passes for history on our television sets, in our newspapers, and in our schools. We were told how the Founding Fathers, in writing the Constitution, gave the state legislators the power to choose electors, who would then choose the president. We were told how rival sets of electors were chosen in three states, and how Samuel Tilden, the

Democrat, had 250,000 more popular votes than the Republican, Rutherford Hayes, and needed only one more electoral vote to win the presidency. But when a special commission, with a bare Republican majority, was set up by Congress to decide the dispute, it gave all three states to Hayes and thus made him president.

This told us a lot about the mechanics of presidential elections and the peculiar circumstances of that one. But it told us nothing about how "The Compromise of 1877," worked out in private meetings between Democrats and Republicans, doomed blacks in the South to semislavery. It told us nothing about how the armies that once fought the Confederacy would be withdrawn from the South and sent West to drive indigenous communities from their ancestral lands. It told us nothing about how Democrats and Republicans would now join in subjecting working people all over the country to ruthless corporate power.

Behind the Tilden-Hayes hullabaloo was a hard reality: the Republican Party, and the Northern industrial-financial interests that dominated it, were no longer interested in the fate of the former slaves. The Fourteenth and Fifteenth Amendments had given blacks a few years of new freedom in which they could vote and be elected to office. But the ex-slaves would be given no land, no resources to give meaning to their political freedom. President Hayes, awarded the election, would make concessions to the Democrats and remove the soldiers who had protected black rights in the South. White supremacy would be restored.

In 1877, the country was in the midst of a depression. Farmers and workers were beginning to rebel against the new economic order and the national government that was giving huge favors to the railroad corporations and the manufacturers. The Northern elite now needed to reconcile with the leaders of the white South. In his classic study of the 1877 compromise, *Reunion and Reaction*, the historian C. Vann Woodward asked: "Could the South be induced to combine with the Northern conservatives and become a prop instead of a menace to the new capitalist order?"

That new order was in trouble. The country had been in a depression since 1873. By 1877, desperation was widespread, and railroad workers went out on strike all over the country. In one of the most violent episodes of class warfare in American history, 100,000 workers were on strike, 1,000 were sent to prison, 100 were killed, and the cities of Chicago and St. Louis were brought to a halt. President Hayes, withdrawing soldiers from the South, used some of those same soldiers to smash the strikes.

Other soldiers would be used in the westward expansion of the United States. Ironically, the man who had been head of the Freedman's Bureau and worked to help ex-slaves get some land of their own, General O. O. Howard, now led troops against American Indians in the Far West.

These were the facts of race and class and western expansion concealed behind the disputed election of 1876. The pretense in disputed elections is that the great conflict is between the two major parties. The reality is that there is a much bigger conflict that the two parties jointly wage against large numbers of Americans who are represented by neither party and against powerless millions around the world.

The ferocity of the contest for the presidency in recent elections conceals the agreement between both parties on fundamentals. The evidence for this statement lies in eight years of the Clinton-Gore administration, whose major legislative accomplishments—destroying welfare, imposing more punitive sentences on criminals, increasing Pentagon spending—were part of the Republican agenda.

The Democrats and the Republicans do not dispute the continued corporate control of the economy. Neither party endorses free national health care, proposes extensive low-cost housing, demands a minimum income for all Americans, or supports a truly progressive income tax to diminish the huge gap between rich and poor. Both support the death penalty and the growth of prisons. Both believe in a large military establishment, in land mines and nuclear weapons and the cruel use of sanctions against the people of Cuba.

Perhaps when, after the next election, the furor dies down over who really won the tennis match and we get over our anger at the referee's calls and the final, disputed score, we will finally break the hypnotic spell of the game and look around. We may then think about whether the ship is slowly going down and whether there are enough lifeboats and what we should do about all that.

10

KILLING PEOPLE TO "SEND A MESSAGE"

B oth Timothy McVeigh, who blew up the Federal Building in Oklahoma City, and the United States government, which executed him for the act, have something in common. They both believe in killing people to "send a message." Timothy McVeigh committed his act outside the law, and thus is called a "terrorist." The United States government, executing him, acted by virtue of a law that provides for the death penalty.

The United States is therefore about two hundred years behind the writers of the European Enlightenment who, in the late eighteenth and early nineteenth centuries, declared their abhorrence of the death penalty.

In 1764, an Italian writer, Cesare Beccaria, wrote *An Essay on Crimes and Punishments*, in which he laid out the argument against capital punishment. The great poet Percy Bysshe Shelley spoke out against it as a great evil. In that same period, the Founding Fathers of the American Revolution, themselves influenced by the ideas of the Enlightenment, cut down drastically on the number of crimes for which the punishment was death; under the British king, the list of crimes calling for capital punishment was enormous.

Karl Marx, in the 1850s, writing for the *New York Tribune*, said that capital punishment "cannot be tolerated in any country calling itself civilized."

And if, as Dostoyevsky said, "The degree of civilization in a society can be judged by entering its prisons," then what is one to say about the degree of civilization in a society that creates "super-max" prisons, Guantánamo Bay detention camps, and death chambers for fellow humans?

There are societies that do not pretend to be "civilized"—military dictatorships and totalitarian states—and execute their victims without ceremony. Then there are nations like the United States, whose claim to be civilized rests on the fact that its punishments are legitimized by a complex set of judicial procedures. This is called "due process," despite the fact that each step in this process is tainted by racial prejudice, class bias, or political discrimination.

The death penalty itself is only one manifestation of the violence directed by the state against those whom it considers dispensable, either because they are poor, nonwhite, or part of a movement that threatens the existing structure of wealth and power. In the case, for instance, of death-row inmate Mumia Abu-Jamal, he embodies all of those expendable characteristics—being poor, black, and a self-proclaimed revolutionary.

The state's death penalty is given holy sanction by the Supreme Court, which pretends that racial prejudice is not a factor in deciding who lives and who dies. This, despite a scholarly study which showed that black men who were found guilty of crimes comparable to those of white men were four times as likely to be executed. The Supreme Court, in 1982, decided a case where a black man was convicted by an all-white jury and every possible black juror had been dismissed on peremptory challenges. The Court concluded that there may well have been race bias but that the bias was not "constitutionally significant."

The Supreme Court also decided, in 1993, that the U.S. Constitution does not protect state prisoners from execution even if there is new evidence of innocence, because of "the very disruptive effect that entertaining claims of actual innocence would have on the need for finality in capital cases."

The execution of Timothy McVeigh dramatizes the link between the terrorism of an individual and the terrorism of war. But there was nothing in the U.S. press or in any public forum pointing to McVeigh's own statement that he learned his moral scruples from the government that executed him.

During the First Gulf War of 1990–91, in which McVeigh fought, the U.S. Air Force dropped a bomb on an air raid shelter in Baghdad, killing more than 600 people, many of them women and children. There had been many bombings of buses, trains, highways, hospitals, and neighborhoods, in which civilians were killed, and which the government described as accidents.

It is not accurate to call them accidents, because if you drop huge numbers of bombs on a city, it is inevitable that innocent people will die. However, in the case of the February 15, 1991, air raid shelter attack, the United States did not, as it usually did in such bombings, call the attack an accident. It said bluntly that the bombing was deliberate and justified this by the claim that the air raid shelter was a communications site.

Reporters who went into the rubble immediately after the bombing found not the slightest evidence to support U.S. claims. And even if it was a communications site, would that justify a massacre (there's no other name for it) of hundreds of men, women, and children? If McVeigh had not been in the infantry but in the air force, and had dropped that bomb, killing more than twice the number he killed in Oklahoma, he would be alive and perhaps have another medal pinned to his chest.

In defending his bombing of the Federal Building, with all those dead and wounded, McVeigh used the term "collateral damage," exactly the words used by our government to describe the deaths of civilians in our bombing of various countries, whether Iraq or Panama or Yugoslavia. My *Webster's Collegiate Dictionary* defines "collateral" as "accompanying or related, but secondary or subordinate." Both McVeigh and the leaders of the United States government considered the toll of human life secondary to whatever else was destroyed, and therefore acceptable.

McVeigh is no longer able to let his demented notion of morality lead to any more deaths. The United States government, on the other hand, is very much alive and is carrying out its demented notion of "national interest" in Iraq and Afghanistan, where the number of civilians killed continues to escalate.

The day after Timothy McVeigh's execution, the *Boston Herald* ran a banner headline on its front page that said, IT's OVER!

But it is not over. Terrorism is the killing of innocent people in order to send a message (those are McVeigh's words and also the words of government spokespeople when our planes have bombed some foreign city). So long as our government engages in terrorism, claiming always that it is done for democracy or freedom or to send a message to some other government, there will be more Timothy McVeighs, following the example.

No, it is not over. Individual acts of terrorism will continue, and they will be called—rightly—fanaticism. Government terrorism, on a much larger scale, will continue, and that will be called "foreign policy." And at home, is not the death penalty a kind of terror waged by the state, one death at a time, an attempt to instill fear and obedience in the population? That is the perverted sense of morality which now rules and will go on ruling, until Americans decide that it will no longer be tolerated.

THE DOUBLE HORROR OF
9/11

The images on television were heartbreaking: people on fire leaping to their deaths from a hundred stories up; people in panic racing from the scene in clouds of dust and smoke.

We knew there must have been thousands of human beings buried under a mountain of debris. We could only imagine the terror among the passengers of the hijacked planes as they contemplated the crash, the fire, the end. Those scenes horrified and sickened me.

Then our political leaders came on television, and I was horrified and sickened again. They spoke of retaliation, of vengeance, of punishment.

We are at war, they said. And I thought: they have learned nothing, absolutely nothing, from the history of the twentieth century, from a hundred years of retaliation, vengeance, war—a hundred years of terrorism and counter-terrorism, of violence met with violence in an unending cycle of stupidity.

We can all feel a terrible anger when we witness such senseless violence. But what do we do with that anger? Do we react with panic, strike out violently and blindly just to show how tough we are? "We shall make no distinction," the president proclaimed, "between terrorists and countries that harbor terrorists."

So we went to war first against Afghanistan and then Iraq,

and have bombed locations in Pakistan and Yemen, inevitably killing innocent people because it is in the nature of bombing—and I say this as a former U.S. Air Force bombardier—to be indiscriminate, to "make no distinction."

We have done that before. It is the old way of thinking, the old way of acting. It has never worked. Reagan bombed Libya, and Bush made war on Iraq, and Clinton bombed Afghanistan and also a pharmaceutical plant in the Sudan to "send a message" to terrorists. And then came the horrors in New York, Washington, Madrid, London, Bali, Egypt, Iraq. Isn't it clear by now that sending a message to terrorists through violence doesn't work, that it only leads to more terrorism?

Haven't we learned anything from the Israeli/Palestinian conflict?

One side accuses the other and attacks, instigating retaliations. That has been going on for years. It doesn't work.

Innocent people die on both sides.

Yes, it is an old way of thinking, and we need new ways. We need to think about the resentment all over the world felt by people who have been the victims of American military action:

In Vietnam, where we carried out terrorizing bombing attacks, using napalm and cluster bombs, on peasant villages.

In Latin America, where we supported dictators and death squads in Chile and El Salvador and Guatemala and Haiti.

In Iraq, where prior to the current war, more than 500,000 children had died as a result of economic sanctions imposed by the United States.

And, perhaps most important for understanding the current situation, in the occupied territories of the West Bank and Gaza, where more than a million Palestinians live under Israel's cruel military occupation, while our government supplies Israel with high-tech weapons, funding, and political cover.

We need to realize that the awful scenes of death and suffering we witnessed on 9/11 have been going on in other parts of the world for a long time, and only now can we begin to know what people have gone through, often as a result of our policies. We need to understand how some of those people will go beyond quiet anger to acts of terrorism.

That doesn't, by any means, justify the terror. Nothing justifies killing innocent people. But we would do well to see what might inspire such violence. And it will not be over until we stop concentrating on punishment and retaliation and think calmly and intelligently about how to address its causes.

We need new ways of thinking.

Hundreds of billions for a military budget have not given us security.

Increased militarization, including sending troops to our border with Mexico, has not given us security. Land mines and a "missile defense shield" will not give us security.

We need to stop sending weapons to countries that oppress other people or their own people. We need to decide against war, no matter what reasons are conjured up by the politicians or the media, because war in our time is always indiscriminate—always a war against innocents, a war against children. War is terrorism, magnified hundreds of times.

How can we prevent future 9/11s? We should take our example not from military and political leaders who shout "retaliate" and "war," but from the doctors, nurses, medical students, firefighters, and police officers who were saving lives in the midst of mayhem, whose first thoughts were not violence but healing, not vengeance but compassion.

AFGHANISTAN

E ver since the awful events of 9/11, newspapers and television reports in the United States have been filled with
news and commentary about the "war on terror." First, it
was the military's "Operation Enduring Freedom" in
Afghanistan, which was advertised as a hunt for al-Qaeda
and Osama Bin Laden. Then it was the invasion of Iraq,
called a campaign of "shock and awe" and given the name
"Operation Iraqi Freedom."

This country has thus initiated wars against two countries,
generating a seemingly endless amount of discussion. But in
all of that analysis and commentary, there has been a glar-
ing, indeed unpardonable omission: a close examination of
the human consequences of those actions.

While the United States was bombing Afghanistan, the
people at the *New York Times* did what should always be
done when a tragedy is reduced to statistics: they gave readers miniature portraits of the human beings known to have
died on September 11, 2001—their names, photos, glim-
mers of their personalities, their idiosyncrasies, how friends
and loved ones remembered them.

As the director of the New-York Historical Society said:
"The peculiar genius of it was to put a human face on
numbers that are unimaginable to most of us. . . . It's so
obvious that every one of them was a person who deserved

to live a full and successful and happy life. You see what was lost."

I was deeply moved, reading those intimate sketches: "A Poet of Bensonhurst . . . A Friend, A Sister . . . Someone to Lean On . . . Laughter, Win or Lose. . . ." I thought to myself: Would those who celebrated the grisly deaths of the people in the Twin Towers and the Pentagon as a blow to symbols of American dominance have second thoughts if they could see, up close, the faces of those who lost their lives?

Then it occurred to me: what if all those Americans who declare their support for the U.S. "war on terror" could see, instead of those elusive symbols—Sheikh Mullah Mohammed Omar, Osama bin Laden, al-Qaeda—the real human beings who are being killed by our bombs? I do believe they would have second thoughts.

Most Americans are normally compassionate people, whose instincts go against war, but who were seduced by early official assurances and who consoled themselves with words like "limited" military action and "measured" response. I think they, too, if confronted with the magnitude of the human suffering caused by U.S. attacks, would have second thoughts.

I do believe most Americans (not those fanatics in the Pentagon and around the country who are willing, like their counterparts in other parts of the world, to kill for a cause) would begin to understand that the wars we are waging are wars on ordinary men, women, and children. And that these human beings die because they happen to live in Afghanistan in villages in the vicinity of "military targets"—always vaguely defined—and that the bombing that destroyed their lives is in no way a war on terror because it has no chance of ending terrorism and is itself a form of terrorism.

How can this be done—this turning of human beings into ciphers? Unlike the vignettes in the *New York Times*, there are no available details about the human beings in Afghanistan who died or were wounded as result of American attacks. Only occasionally are there glimpses of that. One day I saw in the *New York Times* the photo of a ten-year-old boy lying on a hospital cot on the Pakistani-Afghan border, blinded, his arms gone, the victim of a bombing attack.

But that story quickly disappeared. Thousand of civilians in Afghanistan have already been killed as a result of our military operations, and countless thousands more are being wounded, losing limbs, blinded. Often these are children, victims of unexploded land mines, or cluster bombs. But the American people are not told those stories; we are kept ignorant of what the "war on terror" means in human terms. Indeed, at least one television executive (for the Fox network) told his reporters not to emphasize civilian casualties.

Reports of people killed or wounded in Afghanistan are mostly out of sight of the general public (indeed, virtually never reported on U.S. national television, where most Americans get their news) and are so dispersed as to reinforce the idea that the killing of civilians is an infrequent event, an accident, a rare, unfortunate mistake

Listen to the language of the Pentagon: "We cannot confirm the report . . . civilian casualties are inevitable . . . we don't know if they were our weapons . . . it was an accident . . . incorrect coordinates had been entered . . . they are deliberately putting civilians in our bombing targets . . . the village was a legitimate military target . . . it just didn't happen . . . we regret any loss of civilian life."

After reports of the bombing of one village, Pentagon

spokeswoman Victoria Clarke said, "We take extraordinary care. . . . There is unintended damage. There is collateral damage. Thus far, it has been extremely limited." The Agence France-Presse reporter quoting her said: "Refugees arriving in Pakistan suggested otherwise. Several recounted how twenty people, including nine children, had been killed as they tried to flee an attack on the southern Afghan town of Tirin Kot."

Listening to the repeated excuses given by President Bush, Defense Secretary Donald Rumsfeld, and others, one recalls former Chairman of the Joint Chiefs of Staff Colin Powell's reply at the end of the First Gulf War, when questioned about Iraqi casualties: "That is really not a matter I am terribly interested in." If, indeed, a strict definition of the word "deliberate" does not apply to the bombs dropped on the civilians of Afghanistan, then we can offer, thinking back to Powell's statement, an alternate characterization: "a reckless disregard for human life."

The denials of the Pentagon are confidently uttered half a world away in Washington. But there are on-the-spot press reports from the hospitals where the wounded lie, from the Pakistani border, and from the villages where refugees have fled the bombs. If we put these reports together, we get brief glimpses of the human tragedies in Afghanistan: the names of the dead, the villages that were bombed, the words of a father who lost his children, the ages of the children. We would then have to multiply these stories by the hundreds, think of the unreported incidents, and know that the numbers go into the thousands. Early in the war, a professor of economics at the University of New Hampshire, Marc Herold, completed a thorough survey of the press, listing location of the killing, type of weapon used, and sources of information. He reports that the civilian death toll in Afghanistan between October 7, 2001, and March 2002 exceeded 3,500, a sad and startling parallel to the number of people killed in the Twin Towers.

The *New York Times* was able to interrogate friends and family of the people killed in the United States on 9/11, but for the people in Afghanistan, we will have to imagine the hopes and dreams of those who died, especially the children, for whom forty or fifty years of mornings, love, friendship, sunsets, and the sheer exhilaration of being alive have been extinguished by monstrous machines sent over their land by people far away.

When you look beyond the wars initiated by the United States these past few years, and consider the suffering of people in Sudan, in Rwanda, in Sierra Leone, in Cambodia, in Algeria, in Palestine, you find that neither our government nor the media pay much attention. Millions of people, many of them children, have died, or endured mutilation from land mines and cluster bombs. This is a silent terrorism, but the United States has not declared war on that. Their stories are untold.

My intention is not at all to diminish our compassion for the victims of the terrorism of September 11, but to enlarge that compassion to include the victims of all terrorism, in any place, at any time, whether perpetrated by religious fanatics or American politicians.

In that spirit, I present the following news items (only a fraction of those in my files), hoping that there is the patience to go through them, like the patience required to read the portraits of the September 11 dead, like the patience required to read the 58,000 names on the Vietnam Veterans Memorial:

From a hospital in Jalālābād, Afghanistan, John Donnelly reported in the *Boston Globe* on December 5, 2001:

"In one bed lay Noor Mohammad, ten, who was a bundle of bandages. He lost his eyes and hands to the bomb that hit his house after Sunday dinner. Hospital director Guloja Shimwari shook his head at the boy's wounds. 'The United States must be thinking he is Osama,' Shimwari said. 'If he is not Osama, then why would they do this?'"

The report continued:

"The hospital's morgue received seventeen bodies last weekend, and officials here estimate at least eighty-nine civilians were killed in several villages. In the hospital yesterday, a bomb's damage could be chronicled in the life of one family. A bomb had killed the father, Faisal Karim. In one bed was his wife, Mustafa Jama, who had severe head injuries. . . . Around her, six of her children were in bandages. . . . One of them, Zahidullah, 8, lay in a coma."

In the *New York Times* on December 15, 2001, Barry Bearak, reporting from the village of Madoo, Afghanistan, tells of the destruction of fifteen houses and their occupants. "'In the night, as we slept, they dropped the bombs on us,' said Paira Gul, a young man whose eyes were aflame with bitterness. His sisters and their families had perished, he said. . . . The houses were small, the bombing precise. No structure escaped the thundering havoc. Fifteen houses, fifteen ruins. . . . 'Most of the dead are children,' Tor Tul said."

Another *Times* reporter, C. J. Chivers, writing from the village of Charykari on December 12, 2001, reported "a terrifying and rolling barrage that the villagers believe was the payload of an American B-52. . . . The villagers say thirty people died. . . . One man, Muhibullah, forty, led the way through his yard and showed three unexploded cluster bombs he is afraid to touch. A fourth was not a dud. It landed near his porch. 'My son was sitting there . . . the metal went inside him.' The boy, Zumarai, five, is in a hospital in Kunduz, with wounds to leg and abdomen. His sister, Sharpari, ten, was killed. 'The United States killed my daughter and injured my son,' Mr. Muhibullah said. 'Six of my cows were destroyed and all of my wheat and rice was burned. I am very angry. I miss my daughter.'"

Pamela Constable reported from Peshawar, Pakistan, on October 24, 2001, in the *Washington Post*: "Sardar, a taxi driver and father of twelve, said his family had spent night after night listening to the bombing in their community south of Kabul. One night during the first week, he said, a bomb aimed at a nearby radio station struck a house, killing all five members of the family living there. 'There was no sign of a home left,' he said. 'We just collected the pieces of bodies and buried them.'"

Catherine Philp of the *Times* of London reported on October 25, 2001, from Quetta, Pakistan: "It was not long after 7 p.m. on Sunday when the bombs began to fall over the outskirts of Torai village. . . . Rushing outside, Mauroof saw a massive fireball. Morning brought an end to the bombing and . . . a neighbor arrived to tell him that some twenty villagers had been killed in the blasts, among them ten of his relatives. 'I saw the body of one of my brothers-in-law being pulled from the debris,' Mauroof said. 'The lower part of his body had been blown away. Some of the other bodies were unrecognizable. There were heads missing and arms blown off. . . .' The roll call of the dead read like an invitation list to a family wedding: his mother-in-law, two sisters-in-law, three brothers-in-law, and four of his sister's five young children, two girls and two boys, all under the age of eight."

Human Rights Watch reported on October 26, 2001: "Twenty-five-year-old Samiullah . . . rushed home to rescue his family. . . . [H]e found the bodies of his twenty-year-old wife and three of his children: Mohibullah, aged six; Harifullah, aged three; and Bibi Aysha, aged one. . . . Also killed were his two brothers, Nasiullah, aged eight, and Ghaziullah, aged six, as well as two of his sisters, aged fourteen and eleven."

Sayed Salahuddin of Reuters reported on October 28, 2001, from Kabul: "A U.S. bomb flattened a flimsy mud-brick home in Kabul Sunday, blowing apart seven children as they ate breakfast with their father. . . . Sobs racked the body of a middle-aged man as he cradled the head of his baby, its dust-covered body dressed only in a blue diaper, lying beside the bodies of three other children, their colorful clothes layered with debris from their shattered homes."

Washington Post Foreign Service, November 2, 2001, from Quetta, Pakistan, by Rajiv Chandrasekaran:

The thunder of the first explosions jolted Nasir Ahmed awake . . . he grabbed his fourteen-year-old niece and scurried into a communal courtyard. From there, he said, they watched as civilians who survived the bombing run, including his niece and a woman holding her five-year-old son, were gunned down by a slow-moving, propeller-driven aircraft circling overheard. When the gunship departed an hour later, at least twenty-five people in the village—all civilians—were dead, according to accounts of the incident provided today by

Ahmed, two other witnesses, and several relatives
of people in the village.

The Pentagon confirmed that the village was
hit . . . but officials said they believe the aircraft
struck a legitimate military target. . . . Asked about
civilian casualties, the official said, "We don't know.
We're not on the ground."

Shaida, fourteen [said]. . . . "Americans are not
good. . . . They killed my mother. They killed my
father. I don't understand why."

A report from Kabul by James Rupert in *Newsday* on
November 24, 2001, said:

In the sprawling, mud-brick slum of Qala-ye-
Khatir, most men were kneeling in the mosques at
morning prayer on November 6, 2001 when a
quarter-ton of steel and high explosives hurtled
from the sky into the home of Gul Ahmed, a carpet
weaver. The American bomb detonated, killing
Ahmed, his five daughters, one of his wives, and a
son. Next door, it demolished the home of Sahib
Dad and killed two of his children. . . .

Ross Chamberlain, the coordinator for U.N.
mine-clearing operations in much of Afghanistan.
. . . "There's really no such thing as a precision
bombing. . . . We are finding more cases of errant
targeting than accurate targeting, more misses
than hits."

Ghaleh Shafer, reporting for the *New York Times* from
Afghanistan on November 22, 2001, wrote: "10-year-old

Mohebolah Seraj went out to collect wood for his family, and thought he had happened upon a food packet. He picked it up and lost three fingers in an explosion. Doctors say he will probably lose his whole hand . . . [H]is mother, Sardar Seraj . . . said that she cried and told the doctors not to cut off her son's whole hand. . . ."

"The hospital where her son is being cared for is a grim place, lacking power and basic sanitation. In one room lay Muhammad Ayoub, a twenty-year-old who was in the house when the cluster bomb initially landed. He lost a leg and his eyesight, and his face was severely disfigured. He moaned in agony. . . . Hospital officials said that a sixteen-year-old had been decapitated."

On December 3, 2001, Tim Weiner reported the following for the *New York Times* from Jalālābād, Afghanistan:

> The commanders, who are pro-American . . . say that four nearby villages were struck this weekend, leaving eighty or more people dead and others wounded. . . . The villages are near Tora Bora, the mountain camp where Mr. Bin Laden is presumed to be hiding. A Pentagon spokesman said Saturday that the bombing of civilians near Tora Bora "never happened."
>
> "Eight men guarding the building [a district office building] . . . were killed," [*mujahedeen* commander] Hajji Zaman said. He gave the names of the dead as Zia ul-Hassan, sixteen; Wilayat Khan, seventeen; Abdul Wadi, twenty; Jany, twenty-two; Abdul Wahid, thirty; Hajji Wazir, thirty-five; Hajji Nasser, also thirty-five; and Awlia Gul, thirty-seven. . . . Ali Shah, twenty-six, of Landa Khel, said,

"There is no one in this village who is part of Al Qaeda."

Witnesses said that at least fifty and as many as two hundred villagers had been killed.

"We are poor people," [Muhammad] Tahir said. "Our trees are our only shelter from the cold and wind. The trees have been bombed. Our waterfall, our only source of water—they bombed it. Where is the humanity?"

The *Independent* reported the following on December 4, 2001: "The village where nothing happened. . . . The cemetery on the hill contains forty freshly dug graves, unmarked and identical. And the village of Kama Ado has ceased to exist. . . . And all this is very strange because, on Saturday morning—when American B-52s unloaded dozens of bombs that killed 115 men, women and children—nothing happened. . . . We know this because the U.S. Department of Defense told us so. . . . 'It just didn't happen.'"

David Rohde reported the following from Ghazni, Afghanistan, for the *New York Times* on December 12, 2001:

Each ward of the Ghazni Hospital features a new calamity. In the first, two 14-year-old boys had lost parts of their hands when they picked up land mines. "I was playing with a toy and it exploded" said one of them, Muhammad Allah. . . . [A] woman named Rose lay on a bed in the corner of the room, grunting with each breath. Her waif-like children slept nearby, whimpering periodically. Early on Sunday morning, shrapnel from an American bomb tore through the woman's abdomen, broke her four-year-old son's leg and ripped into her six-year-old daughter's head, doctors here said. A second six-year-old girl in the room was paralyzed from the waist down. X-rays showed how a tiny shard of metal had neatly severed her spinal cord.

The following was reported in the *Chicago Tribune*, December 28, 2001, by Paul Salopek, from Madoo, Afghanistan: "'American soldiers came after the bombing and asked if any Al Qaeda had lived here,' said villager Paira Gul. 'Is that an Al Qaeda?' Gul asked, pointing to a child's severed foot he had excavated minutes earlier from a smashed house. 'Tell me,' he said, his voice choking with fury, 'is that what an Al Qaeda looks like?'"

A Reuters report dated December 31, 2001, from Qalaye Niazi, Afghanistan: "Janat Gul said twenty-four members of his family were killed in the pre-dawn U.S. bombing raid on Qalaye Niazi, and described himself as the sole survivor. . . . In the U.S. Major Pete Mitchell—a spokesman for U.S. Central Command—said: 'We are aware of the incident and we are currently investigating.'"

Yes, these reports appeared, but scattered through the first months of bombing Afghanistan and on the inside pages, or buried in larger stories and accompanied by solemn government denials. With scarce access to alternative and independent sources of information, it is not surprising that a majority of Americans have approved of what they have been led to think is a "war on terror."

In World War I there was a ten-to-one ratio of military personnel killed versus civilians, whereas in World War II that ratio became 60 percent civilians, 40 percent military. Since World War II, a vast majority of the people who have gotten killed in wars have been civilians. Gino Strada, the Italian war surgeon who has operated on war victims all over the world these last ten years, estimates that 90 percent are civilians, one-third children.

And by the way, I don't want to insist on the distinction between innocent civilians and soldiers who are not innocent. The Iraqi soldiers whom we crushed with bulldozers, toward the end of the First Gulf War in 1991, in what way were they not innocent? The U.S. Army just buried them—buried them—hundreds and hundreds and hundreds of them. What of the Iraqi soldiers the United States mowed down in the so-called Turkey Shoot as they were retreating, already defeated? Who were these soldiers on the other side? They weren't Saddam Hussein. They were just poor young men who had been conscripted.

I suggest that the history of bombing—and no one has bombed more than this nation—is a history of endless atrocities, all calmly explained by deceptive and deadly language like "accident," "military targets," and "collateral damage."

Indeed, in both World War II and in Vietnam, the historical record shows that there was a deliberate decision to target civilians in order to destroy the morale of the enemy: hence the firebombing of Dresden, Hamburg, Tokyo, the B-52s over Hanoi, the jet bombers over peaceful villages in the Vietnam countryside. When some argue that we can engage in "limited military action" without "an excessive use of force," they are ignoring the history of bombing. The momentum of war rides roughshod over limits.

The moral equation in Afghanistan is clear. Civilian casualties are high, but the outcome is uncertain. No one knows what years of U.S. military attacks and occupation will accomplish—whether it will lead to the capture of Sheik Mullah Omar and Osama bin Laden (perhaps), or the permanent end of the Taliban (possibly), or a democratic Afghanistan (very unlikely), or an end to terrorism (almost certainly not).

In the meantime we are terrorizing the population of Afghanistan (not the terrorists; they are not easily terrorized). Hundreds of thousands packed their belongings onto carts and with their children left behind their homes to make dangerous journeys to places they thought might be safer.

In his book *Imperial Hubris*, former senior CIA terrorism analyst Michael Scheuer says bluntly that U.S. policies—supporting Israel, making war on Afghanistan and Iraq—"are completing the radicalization of the Islamic world."

Unless we reexamine our policies—our quartering of soldiers in a hundred countries (the quartering of foreign soldiers, remember, was one of the grievances of the American revolutionaries), our support of the Israeli occupation of Palestinian lands, our insistence on controlling the oil of the Middle East—we will always be incensing others to attack us. If we were to announce that we will reconsider those policies, and began to change them, we might start to dry up the huge reservoir of hatred from which terrorists spring.

13

PACIFISM AND WAR

With the world immersed in the turmoil of war, it may be useful to examine the idea of pacifism. I have never used the word "pacifist" to describe myself, because it suggests something absolute, and I am suspicious of absolutes. I want to leave openings for unpredictable possibilities. There might be situations—and even such strong pacifists as Gandhi and Martin Luther King believed this—when a small, focused act of violence against a monstrous, immediate evil would be justified.

In war, however, the proportion of means to ends is very, very different. War, by its nature, is unfocused, indiscriminate, and, especially in our time when the technology is so murderous, inevitably involves the deaths of large numbers of people and the suffering of even more. Even in "small wars" (Iran-Iraq War, the Nigerian war, the Afghan war), a million people die. Even in a "tiny" war like the one we waged in Panama, a thousand or more die.

Scott Simon of National Public Radio wrote a commentary in the *Wall Street Journal* on October 11, 2001, entitled "Even Pacifists Must Support This War." He tried to use the pacifist acceptance of self-defense, which approves a focused resistance to an immediate attacker, to justify the U.S. invasion of Afghanistan, which he claims is "self-defense." But the term "self-defense" does not apply when you drop bombs all over a country and kill lots of people other than your attacker. And it doesn't apply when there is no likelihood that the action will achieve its desired end.

Pacifism, which I define as a rejection of war, rests on a very powerful logic. In war, the means—indiscriminate killing—are immediate and certain; the ends, however desirable, are distant and uncertain.

Pacifism does not mean "appeasement." That word was often hurled at those who condemned the present wars on Afghanistan and Iraq, and was accompanied by references to Churchill, Chamberlain, and Munich. World War II analogies, however irrelevant to a particular situation, are conveniently summoned when there is a need to justify a war. At the suggestion that we withdraw from Vietnam, or not invade Iraq, the word "appeasement" was bandied about.

Let's examine that analogy. Czechoslovakia was handed to the voracious Hitler to "appease" him. Germany was an aggressive nation expanding its power, and to help it in its expansion was not wise. But today we do not face an expansionist power that demands to be appeased. We ourselves are the expansionist power—at war in two countries, troops stationed around the world, naval vessels on every sea—and that, along with Israel's expansion into the West Bank and Gaza Strip, arouses perpetual anger.

It was wrong to give up Czechoslovakia to appease Hitler. It is not wrong to withdraw our military from the Middle East, or for Israel to withdraw from the occupied territories, because there is no right to be there. That would not be appeasement. That would be justice.

Opposing the U.S. wars in Afghanistan and Iraq does not constitute "giving in to terrorism" or "appeasement." It asks that other means than war be found to solve the problems that confront us. King and Gandhi both believed in action—nonviolent direct action, which is more powerful and certainly more morally defensible than war.

To reject war is not to "turn the other cheek," as pacifism has been caricatured. It is, in the present instance, to act in ways that do not imitate the terrorists.

The United States could have treated the September 11 attacks as horrific criminal acts that called for apprehending the culprits, using every device of intelligence and investigation possible. It could have gone to the United Nations to enlist the aid of other countries in the pursuit and apprehension of those who were responsible.

There was also the avenue of negotiations. (And let's not hear: "What? Negotiate with those monsters?" The United States negotiated with—indeed, brought into power and kept in power—some of the most monstrous governments in the world.) Before Bush gave the order to bomb, the Taliban offered to put bin Laden on trial. This was ignored. After ten days of air attacks, when the Taliban called for a halt to the bombing and said they would be willing to talk about handing bin Laden to a third country for trial, the headline in the *New York Times* the next day read: PRESIDENT REJECTS OFFER BY TALIBAN FOR NEGOTIATIONS, and Bush was quoted as saying: "When I said no negotiations, I meant no negotiations."

President Bush has behaved like someone hell-bent on war. There were similar rejections of negotiating possibilities at the start of the Korean War, the war in Vietnam, the First Gulf War, and the bombing of Yugoslavia. The result was an immense loss of life and incalculable human suffering.

International police work and negotiations were alternatives to war. But let's not deceive ourselves; even if we succeeded in apprehending bin Laden or, as is unlikely, destroying the entire al-Qaeda network, that would not end the threat of terrorism, which has potential recruits far beyond al-Qaeda. As we see in Iraq, killing Abu Musab al-Zarqawi, the mastermind behind hundreds of bombings, has done nothing to slow the pace of car bombs and suicide attacks there. In fact, violence has escalated.

Getting at the roots of terrorism is complicated. Dropping bombs is simple. It is an old response to what everyone acknowledges is a very new situation. At the core of unspeakable and unjustifiable acts of terrorism are justified grievances felt by millions of people who would not themselves engage in terrorism but from whose ranks violent desperation springs.

Those grievances are of two kinds: the existence of profound misery—hunger, illness—in much of the world, contrasted to the wealth and luxury of the West, especially the United States; and the presence of American military power everywhere in the world, propping up oppressive regimes and repeatedly intervening with force to maintain U.S. hegemony.

This suggests actions that not only deal with the long-term problem of terrorism but also are in themselves just.

We need to immediately end the U.S. occupation of Iraq, which has already killed at least tens of thousands of civilians and which has not brought "democracy" but greater destabilization to the entire region.

We must also insist that Israel withdraw from the occupied territories, something that many Israelis also think is right and which would make Israel more secure than it is now.

Let us be a more modest nation; we will then be more secure. The modest nations of the world don't face the threat of terrorism. In short, let us cease being a military superpower, and start becoming a humanitarian superpower.

Such fundamental changes in foreign policy are hardly to be expected. They would threaten too many interests: the power of political leaders, the ambitions of the military, and the profits that corporations gain from the nation's enormous military commitments.

Change will come, as at other times in our history, only when American citizens—becoming better informed, having second thoughts after the first instinctive support for official policy—demand it. That change in citizen opinion, especially if it coincides with a pragmatic decision by the government that its violence isn't working, could bring about a retreat from the military solution.

It might also be a first step in the rethinking of our nation's role in the world. Such a rethinking contains the promise, for Americans, of genuine security, and for people elsewhere, the beginning of hope.

14

THE BOSTON MASSACRE

I was recently invited to participate in a symposium in Boston at historic Faneuil Hall (named after a slave trader but the site of many abolitionist meetings). The topic was going to be the Boston Massacre. I hesitated a moment at the invitation, then said, yes, I would speak, but only if I could also speak about other massacres in American history.

It was clear to me that the Boston Massacre, which took place on March 5, 1770, when British troops killed five colonists, is a much-remembered—indeed, overremembered—event. Even the word "massacre" is a bit of an exaggeration; *Webster's Collegiate Dictionary* says the word denotes "wholesale slaughter."

Still, there is no denying the ugliness of a militia firing into a crowd, using as its rationale the traditional claim of trigger-happy police—that the crowd was "unruly" (as it undoubtedly was). John Adams, who was defense lawyer for the British soldiers and secured their acquittal, described the crowd as "a motley rabble of saucy boys, Negroes and mulattos, Irish teagues and outlandish jack tarrs."

Adams could hardly have expressed more clearly that the race and class of the victims (one of the dead, Crispus Attucks, was a mulatto) made their lives less precious. This was only one of many instances in which the Founding Fathers registered their desire to keep revolutionary fervor under the control of the more prosperous classes.

Ten thousand Bostonians (out of a total population of

16,000) marched in the funeral procession for the victims of the Massacre. And the British, hoping not to provoke more anger, pulled their troops out of Boston. Undoubtedly, the incident helped build sentiment for independence.

Still, I wanted to discuss other massacres because it seemed to me that concentrating attention on the Boston Massacre would be a painless exercise in patriotic fervor. There is no surer way to obscure the deep divisions of race and class in American history than by uniting us in support of the American Revolution and all its symbols—like Paul Revere's stark etching of the soldiers shooting into the crowd.

I suggested to the people assembled at Faneuil Hall (the walls around us crowded with portraits of the Founding Fathers and the nation's military heroes) that there were other massacres, forgotten or dimly remembered, that deserved to be recalled. These ignored episodes could tell us much about racial hysteria and class struggle, about shameful moments in our continental and overseas expansion, so that we can see ourselves more clearly and honestly.

Why, for instance, was there not a symposium on what we might call "The Taino Massacre," perpetrated by Columbus and his fellow conquistadors—which annihilated the native population of Hispaniola? Before they arrived, there were several million living on that island. By 1550, perhaps only 50,000 were left on the island, which is now shared by Haiti and the Dominican Republic.

Why not organize a public forum on "the Pequot Massacre" of 1636, when our Puritan ancestors (well, I am stretching my ancestry a little), in an expedition led by Captain John Mason, set fire to a village of Pequot Indians on the Connecticut shore of Long Island Sound? Here's how William Bradford, an early settler, described the attack in his *History of Plymouth Plantation*:

> Those that scaped the fire, were slaine with the sword; some hewed to peeces, others run through with their rapiers, so as they were quickly dispatchte and very few escaped. It was conceived they thus destroyed about 400, at this time. It was a fearfull sight to see them thus frying in the fyre, and the streams of blood quenching the same, and horrible was the stinck and sente ther of; they gave the prays thereof to God, who had wrought so wonderfully for them, thus to inclose their enemies in their hands, and give them so speedy a victory over so proud and insulting an enimie.

"It was supposed that no less than 600 Pequot souls were brought down to hell that day," wrote the Puritan theologian Cotton Mather, an expert on the destination of souls.

The massacres of American Indians by the armies of the United States—in Colorado in 1864, in Montana in 1870, in South Dakota in 1890, to cite just a few—were massacres in the most literal sense: that is, wholesale slaughter in each case of hundreds of unarmed men, women, and children. The number of those events cannot be counted, and should by that fact be a subject for intense scrutiny.

The results of such an investigation would be as sobering to young Americans as the story of the Boston Massacre is inspiring. And sobriety about our national sins (sorry to use Dr. Mather's terminology) might be very instructive at a time when we need to consider what role we will play in the world this next century.

Atrocities against African Americans took place either by official acts, or by white mobs, with the collaboration of government officials. In the summer of 1917, an article called "The Massacre of East Louis" appeared in the NAACP publication, *Crisis*, written by W. E. B. DuBois and Martha Gruening. When African Americans were hired to replace whites, hysteria took hold. (Job desperation was a common cause of mob violence, as when whites attacked Chinese miners in Rock Spring, Wyoming, in 1885, killing twenty-five.) The black section of East St. Louis became the object of attack by a white mob, leaving six thousand blacks homeless and perhaps two hundred dead. Mangled bodies were found floating in the Mississippi River. Josephine Baker, the St. Louis–born entertainer who decided she could not live in this country, said at the time: "The very idea of America makes me shake and tremble and gives me nightmares."

Other African Americans protested. In New York City, thousands marched silently down Fifth Avenue to the roll of drums, with signs addressed to President Woodrow Wilson: *Mr. President, why not make America safe for democracy?*

The killing of workers by police and militia is given little notice in our history books. I thought I knew about many of these events, but I keep learning about more. I did not know until recently (that is, until I was invited to join in a recollection of the event) about the Bay View Massacre in Milwaukee, which took place May 5, 1886 (the day after the Haymarket bombing in Chicago). On that day, striking steel workers marched toward a mill in the Bay View section of Milwaukee and were intercepted by a squad of militia who fired point-blank into the strikers, killing seven.

A year later, in the fall of 1897, there was a coal strike in

Pennsylvania. Immigrant Austrians, Hungarians, Italians, and Germans were brought in to break the strike. But the strikebreakers themselves soon organized and went on strike. Marching toward the Lattimer mine, they refused to disperse. The sheriff and his deputies opened fire, and killed nineteen people, most of them shot in the back.

When, the following year, the press set out to create a national excitement over the mysterious sinking of the battleship *Maine* in Havana harbor, a machinists' journal pointed to the Lattimer Massacre, saying that the deaths of workers resulted in no such uproar. It pointed out that "the carnival of carnage that takes place every day, month and year in the realm of industry, the thousands of useful lives that are annually sacrificed to the Moloch of greed . . . brings forth no shout for vengeance and reparation."

In 1919, a mob attack in Elaine, Arkansas, left 73 African Americans dead. In 1921, in Tulsa, Oklahoma, planes dropped nitroglycerin on a 36-block black business district, destroying hundreds of businesses, more than a thousand homes, twenty churches, a hospital, libraries, and schools. The number of black people killed was estimated by some in the hundreds, by others in the thousands, with bodies put into mass graves, stuffed into mine shafts or thrown into the river.

Better known, but still absent from mainstream history books, is the Ludlow Massacre of 1914. Two companies of National Guardsmen, their pay underwritten by the Rockefeller interests that owned the Colorado Fuel & Iron Corporation, launched a military attack on the miners' tent colony, where 1,000 men, women, and children lived. The Guardsmen poured machine-gun fire into the tents, then burned them. Eleven children and two women died in the conflagration.

One of the many strikes of the Depression years was against Republic Steel in Chicago in 1937. Police began firing at a picket line and continued firing as the workers fled, killing ten in what came to be known as the Memorial Day Massacre.

Even less likely to enter the history books are the atrocities the United States commits overseas. High school and college texts usually deal at length with the three-month Spanish-American War, portraying the United States as liberating Cuba from Spain and admiring Theodore Roosevelt's exploits with the "Rough Riders." But they rarely pay attention to the eight-year war to conquer the Philippines, a bloody affair that in many ways resembled the war in Vietnam. The United States killed hundreds of thousands of Filipinos in the war, but U.S. casualties were under 5,000.

In 1906, an American military detachment attacked a village of Filipino Muslims ("Moros") living in the hollow of a mountain on one of the southern islands. Every one of 600 men, women, and children were killed. This was the Moro Massacre, which drew an angry response from Mark Twain and other anti-imperialist Americans.

In his capacity as vice president of the Anti-Imperialist League, Twain wrote: "We have pacified thousands of the islanders and buried them, destroyed their fields, burned their villages, turned their widows and orphans out-of-doors, furnished heartbreak by exile to dozens of disagreeable patriots, and subjugated the remaining ten million by Benevolent Assimilation."

Those of us who were of age during the Vietnam War remember the My Lai Massacre of 1968, in which a company of American soldiers poured automatic rifle fire into groups of unarmed villagers, killing perhaps 500 people, many of them women and children. But when I spoke recently to a group of a hundred high school honors students in history and asked who knew about the My Lai Massacre, no one raised their hand.

My Lai was not a unique event. A U.S. Army colonel charged with covering up the My Lai incident told reporters: "Every unit of brigade size has its My Lai hidden someplace."

And if the word "massacre" means indiscriminate mass slaughter of innocent people, is it not reasonable to call the bombings of Hiroshima and Nagasaki "massacres," as well as the firebombing of Tokyo and the destruction of Dresden and other German cities?

And what of the massacre at Attica Prison in New York State in 1971, when Governor Nelson D. Rockefeller ordered the National Guard to attack a prison yard taken over by rebellious prisoners trying to negotiate improvements in their conditions? Thirty-one prisoners, who had no guns, and nine hostages, were shot to death by the militia.

And then there are the police assaults on the homes of people who are deemed expendable for one reason or another—the black families known as MOVE in Philadelphia; a bomb dropped on them by police helicopter; a fire engulfing the neighborhood; eleven people, most of them children, killed. And the military attack, approved by the Clinton administration, on a recalcitrant religious sect in Waco, Texas, resulting in the deaths of eighty-one men, women, and children.

In Ignazio Silone's novel *Fontamara* about peasants living under Italian fascism, an underground resistance movement produces leaflets in order to disseminate information that had been suppressed and then simply to ask: "*Che fare?*"—"What shall we do?" ("They have killed Berardo Viola. What shall we do? They have taken away our water. What shall we do? They violate our women in the name of the law. What shall we do?")

When our government, our media, and our institutions of higher learning select certain events for remembering and ignore others, we have the responsibility to supply the missing information. Just telling untold truths has a powerful effect, for people with ordinary common sense may then begin asking themselves and others: "What shall we do?"

15

RESPECTING THE HOLOCAUST

During the mid-1980s, when I was teaching at Boston University, I was asked by a Jewish group to give a talk on the Holocaust. I spoke that evening, but not about the Holocaust of World War II, the genocide of 6 million Jews. At the time the U.S. government was supporting death squads in Central America, so I spoke of the deaths of hundreds of thousands of peasants in Guatemala and El Salvador, victims of American policy.

My point was that the memory of the Jewish Holocaust should not be encircled by barbed wire, morally ghettoized, kept isolated from other atrocities in history. To remember what happened to the 6 million Jews, I said, served no important purpose unless it aroused indignation, anger, and action against all atrocities, anywhere in the world.

A few days later, in the campus newspaper, there was a letter from a faculty member who had heard me speak. He was a Jewish refugee who had left Europe for Argentina and then the United States. He objected strenuously to my extending the moral issue from Jews in Europe during the war to people in other parts of the world in our time. The Holocaust was a sacred memory, a unique event, he said. And he was outraged that, invited to speak on the Jewish Holocaust, I had chosen to speak about other matters.

I was reminded of this experience when I recently read a

book by Peter Novick, *The Holocaust in American Life.*
Novick's starting point is the following question: why, more
than fifty years after the event, does the Holocaust play a
more prominent role in this country—Holocaust Museums
in Washington and Manhattan, hundreds of Holocaust programs in schools—than it did in the first decades after
World War II?

At the core of the memory of the Holocaust is a horror
that should not be forgotten. But around that core, whose
integrity needs no enhancement, there has grown up an
industry of memorialists who have labored to keep that
memory alive for purposes of their own, Novick points out.

Some Jews have used the Holocaust as a way of preserving a unique identity, which they see threatened by intermar-
riage and assimilation.

Zionists have used the Holocaust, since the 1967 war, to
justify further Israeli expansion into Palestinian land and to
build support for a beleaguered Israel (more beleaguered—
as David Ben-Gurion, Israel's first prime minister, predicted—once it occupied the West Bank and Gaza).

And non-Jewish politicians have used the Holocaust to
curry favor with the numerically small but influential
Jewish voters—note the solemn pronouncements of presidents wearing yarmulkes to accentuate their anguished
sympathy.

All who have taken seriously the admonition "Never
Again" must ask ourselves—as we observe the horrors
around us in the world—if we have used that phrase as a
beginning or as an end to our moral concern.

I would not have become a historian if I thought that it
would become my professional duty to never emerge from
the past, to study long-gone events and remember them

only for their uniqueness, not connecting them to events going on in our time.

If the Holocaust is to have any meaning, we must transfer our anger to today's brutalities. We must respect the memory of the Jewish Holocaust by refusing to allow atrocities to take place now.

When Jews turn inward to concentrate on their own history and look away from the ordeal of others, they are, with terrible irony, doing exactly what the rest of the world did in allowing the genocide to happen.

There have been shameful moments, travesties of Jewish humanism, as when Jewish organizations lobbied against congressional recognition of the Armenian Holocaust of 1915 on the ground that it diluted the memory of the Jewish Holocaust. The designers of the Holocaust Museum dropped the idea of mentioning the Armenian genocide as a result of pressure from the Israeli government, among others.

Another such moment came when Elie Wiesel, chair of President Carter's Commission on the Holocaust, refused to include in a description of the Holocaust Hitler's killing of millions of non-Jews. That would be, he said, to "falsify" the reality "in the name of misguided universalism," Novick quotes Wiesel as saying. "They are stealing the Holocaust from us." As a result, the Holocaust Museum gave only passing mention to the *5 million* or more non-Jews who were killed in the Nazi camps.

To build a wall around the uniqueness of the Jewish Holocaust is to abandon the idea that humankind is all one, that we are all—of whatever color, nationality, religion—deserving of equal rights to life, liberty, and the pursuit of happiness. What happened to the Jews under Hitler is unique in its details, but it shares universal characteristics with many other events in human history: the Atlantic slave trade, the genocide against American Indians, and the injuries and deaths to millions of working people who were victims of the capitalist ethos that put profit before human life.

In recent years, while paying more and more homage to the Holocaust as a central symbol of people's cruelty to other people, we have, by silence and inaction, collaborated in an endless chain of cruelties.

There have been the massacres of Rwanda, and the starvation in Somalia, with our government watching and doing nothing.

There were the death squads in Latin America and the decimation of the population of East Timor, with our government actively collaborating. Our churchgoing Christian presidents, so pious in their references to the genocide against the Jews, kept supplying the instruments of death to the perpetrators of these atrocities.

I am reminded of the last stanza of the poem "Scottsboro, Too, Is Worth Its Song," by Countee Cullen:

> *Surely, I said*
> *now will the poets sing.*
> *But they have raised no cry.*
> *I wonder why.*

Then there are horrors that are not state-sponsored but still take a biblical toll, horrors that are within our power to end. Paul Farmer describes these in detail in his remarkable book, *Infections and Inequalities: The Modern Plagues.* He notes the deaths of 10 million children all over the world who die every year of malnutrition and preventable diseases.

The World Health Organization estimates that each year, 2 million people die of tuberculosis, which is preventable and curable, as Farmer has proved in his medical work in Haiti. With a small portion of our military budget we could wipe out that disease.

My point is not to diminish the experience of the Jewish Holocaust, but to enlarge upon it.

For Jews, it means to reclaim the tradition of Jewish universal humanism against an Israel-centered nationalism. Or, as Novick puts it, to go back to "that larger social consciousness that was the hallmark of the American Jewry of my youth." That larger consciousness is displayed today by those Israelis like Tanya Reinhart who protest Israel's violence against Lebanon and who have resisted the building of the Israeli wall deep into Palestinian lands, the bulldozing of homes and olive groves as collective punishment, and massacres like the one that took place in the Jenin refugee camp.

For others, whether Armenians or American Indians or Africans or Bosnians, it means to use their own bloody histories not to set themselves apart from others but to create a larger solidarity against the holders of wealth and power, the perpetrators and collaborators of the ongoing horrors of our time.

The Holocaust might serve a powerful purpose if it led us to think of the world today as wartime Germany—where millions die while the rest of the population obediently goes about its business. It is a frightening thought that the Nazis, in defeat, were victorious: today Germany, tomorrow the world. That is, until we reverse our obedience and resist.

16

PATRIOTISM

S ometime in the 1960s the folk singer Tom Paxton wrote
a song called "What Did You Learn in School Today?"
The song includes the following lines:

> *I learned that Washington never told a lie,*
> *I learned that soldiers seldom die. . . .*
> *I learned our government must be strong,*
> *It's always right and never wrong.*

The song is amusing—an exaggeration, of course—but
not too far off the mark for all of us who grew up in the
United States and were taught to have pride in our nation
as soon as we entered public school. So much of our early
education is filled with stories and images coming out of
the Revolutionary War: the Boston Tea Party, Paul Revere,
the battle of Bunker Hill, Washington crossing the
Delaware, the heroism of soldiers at Valley Forge, the making of the Constitution. Our history is suffused with emotional satisfaction, glorying in the military victories, proud
of our national leaders.

The march across the continent that follows the Revolution
is depicted on classroom maps as the Westward Expansion.
The phrase suggests a kind of natural, almost biological
growth, not mentioning the military forays into Spanish
Florida, the armed aggression against Mexico, and the massacres and forced removals of the indigenous peoples. Instead

the maps are colored and labeled with different events using benign language: "Louisiana Purchase," "Florida Purchase," "Mexican Cession." Commercial transactions and generous gifts, rather than military occupation and conquest.

Young people learning such a "patriotic" history would easily conclude that, as Tom Paxton's song puts it, our government is "always right and never wrong." And if so, it is our duty to support whatever our government does, even to be willing to give our lives in war. But is that patriotism in the best sense of the word? If patriotism means supporting your government's policies without question, then we are on our way to a totalitarian state.

Patriotism in a democratic society cannot possibly be unquestioning support of the government, not if we take seriously the principles of democracy as set forth in the Declaration of Independence, our founding document. The Declaration makes a clear distinction between the government and the people. Governments are artificial creations, the Declaration says, established by the people with the obligation to protect certain ends: the equal rights of all to "Life, Liberty, and the pursuit of Happiness." And "whenever any form of Government becomes destructive of these ends, it is the Right of the People to alter or abolish it. . . ."

Surely, if it is the right of the people to "alter or abolish," it is their right to criticize, even severely, policies they believe destructive of the ends for which government has been established. This principle, in the Declaration of Independence, suggests that a true patriotism lies in supporting the values the country is supposed to cherish: equality, life, liberty, the pursuit of happiness. When our government compromises, undermines, or attacks those values, it is being unpatriotic.

That characterization of governments expressed in the Declaration, as "deriving their just Powers from the consent of the governed" has been understood by the most heroic of Americans—not the heroes of war, but the heroes of the long struggle for social justice. Mark Twain was one of many who distinguished between the country and the government.

Several years before he denounced the U.S. invasion of the Philippines, Mark Twain had written the novel *A Connecticut Yankee in King Arthur's Court* and put into the mouth of his main character these words:

> You see my kind of loyalty was loyalty to one's country, not to its institutions or its officeholders. The country is the real thing, the substantial thing, the eternal thing; it is the thing to watch over, and care for, and be loyal to; institutions are extraneous, they are its mere clothing, and clothing can wear out, become ragged, cease to be comfortable, cease to protect the body from winter, disease and death. To be loyal to rags, to shout for rags, to worship rags, to die for rags—that is a loyalty of unreason, it is pure animal; it belongs to monarchy, was invented by monarchy; let monarchy keep it.

The same distinction between government and country was made in the years before World War I by the feminist-anarchist Emma Goldman, who lectured in many cities on the subject of patriotism:

> What is patriotism? Is it love of one's birthplace, the place of childhood's recollections and hopes, dreams

PATRIOTISM

and aspirations? Is it the place where, in childlike naivety, we would watch the fleeting clouds, and wonder why we, too, could not run so swiftly? ... Indeed, conceit, arrogance, and egotism are the essentials of patriotism. Patriotism assumes that our globe is divided into little spots, each one surrounded by an iron gate. Those who have had the fortune of being born on some particular spot, consider themselves better, nobler, grander, more intelligent than the living beings inhabiting any other spot. It is, therefore, the duty of everyone living on that chosen spot to fight, kill, and die in the attempt to impose his superiority upon all the others.

Defining patriotism as obedience to government—as an uncritical acceptance of any war the leaders of government decide must be fought—has been disastrous for the American people. Failure to distinguish between the country and the government has led so many young people, recruited into the military, to declare that that they would be willing to die for their country. Would not those young people hesitate before enlisting if they considered that they were not risking their lives for their country, but for the government, and even for the owners of great wealth, the giant corporations connected to the government?

As a patriot, contemplating the dead GIs in Afghanistan and Iraq, I could comfort myself (as, understandably, their families do) with the thought: "They died for their country." But I would be lying to myself.

Today, the U.S. soldiers who are being killed in Iraq and Afghanistan are not dying for their country; they are dying for their government. They are dying for Cheney, Bush, and Rumsfeld. And yes, they are dying for the greed of the oil cartels, for the expansion of the American empire, for the political ambitions of the president. They are dying to cover up the theft of the nation's wealth to pay for the machines of death. As of July 4, 2006, more than 2,500 U.S. soldiers have been killed in Iraq, and almost 20,000 have been maimed or injured.

It is the country that is primary—the people, the ideals of the sanctity of human life, and the promotion of liberty. When a government recklessly expends the lives of its young for crass motives of profit and power, always claiming that its motives are pure and moral ("Operation Just Cause" in the invasion of Panama and "Operation Enduring Freedom" and "Operation Iraqi Freedom" in the present instance), it is violating its promise to the country. War is almost always a breaking of that promise. It does not enable the pursuit of happiness but brings despair and grief.

Mark Twain derided what he called "monarchical patriotism." In his words,

> The gospel of the monarchical patriotism is: "The King can do no wrong." We have adopted it with all its servility, with an unimportant change in the wording: "Our country, right or wrong!" We have thrown away the most valuable asset we had—the individual's right to oppose both flag and country when he believed them to be in the wrong. We have thrown it away; and with it, all that was really respectable about that grotesque and laughable word, Patriotism.

With the United States imposing its might in Iraq and Afghanistan, shall we revel in American military power and—against the history of modern empires—insist that the American empire will be beneficent?

Our own history shows something different. Obedience to whatever the government decides is founded on the idea that the interests of the government are the same as the interests of its citizens. However, we have a long history of government policy that suggests that America's political leaders have had interests different from those of the people. The men who gathered in Philadelphia in 1787 to draft the Constitution, while they drafted provisions for a certain degree of representative government and agreed to a Bill of Rights, did not represent the interests of people forced to be slaves, people whose enslavement was in fact legitimized by the Constitution. Nor did they represent the interests of working people, American Indians, and women of any color or class.

Nor did they represent the average white man of that time—the small farmer—for they intended to fashion a government that would be capable of putting down the kind of rebellions of farmers that had been erupting all over the country in the year before the Constitutional Convention. The very term we use, "Founding Fathers," suggests a family, with common interests. But from the founding of the nation to the present day, the government has generally legislated on behalf of the wealthy, has done the bidding of corporations in dealing with working people, and has taken the nation to war in the interests of economic expansion and political ambition.

It then becomes crucial for democracy to understand this difference of interest between government and people and to see expressions like "the national interest," "national security," "national defense" as ways of obscuring that difference and of enticing the citizens into subservience to power. It becomes important, then, to be wary of those symbols of nationhood which attempt to unite us in a false "patriotism" that works against the interests of the country and its people.

It is not surprising that African Americans, conscious of their status in a white-dominated society, would be more skeptical of such symbols. Frederick Douglass, a former slave who became a leader of the abolitionist movement, was asked in 1852 to speak at a Fourth of July gathering in Rochester, New York. Here is a small sample of what he had to say:

> Fellow citizens, pardon me, allow me to ask, why am I called upon to speak here today? What have I, or those I represent, to do with your national independence? Are the great principles of political freedom and of natural justice, embodied in that Declaration of Independence, extended to us? And am I, therefore, called upon to bring our humble offering to the national altar, and to confess the benefits and express devout gratitude for the blessings resulting from your independence to us? . . .
>
> What, to the American slave, is your 4th of July? I answer; a day that reveals to him, more than all other days in the year, the gross injustice and cruelty to which he is the constant victim. To him, your celebration is a sham; your boasted liberty, an unholy license; your national greatness, swelling vanity . . . your shouts of liberty and equality, hollow mockery . . . a thin veil to cover up crimes which would disgrace a nation of savages. There is

not a nation on the earth guilty of practices more shocking and bloody than are the people of the United States, at this very hour.

African Americans have always had an ambivalent attitude toward the idea of patriotism. They have wanted to feel patriotic in the best sense of the term, that is, to feel at one with their fellow Americans, to feel part of a greater community. And yet, they have resented—while they have endured slavery, lynching, segregation, humiliation, and economic injustice—attempts to enmesh them in a false sense of common interest.

Thus, their reaction to the nation's wars has been a troubled one. The complexity is illustrated by the dramatically different reactions of two boxing champions in two different wars. There was Joe Louis, who was used by the U.S. government to build black support for World War II, saying that whatever was wrong in this country, "Hitler won't fix it." And there was Muhammad Ali, who refused to be drafted for the Vietnam War and told a reporter who challenged him on the war:

"No, I'm not going 10,000 miles from home to help murder and burn another poor nation simply to continue the domination of white slave masters of the darker people the world over. . . . The real enemy of my people is here. . . . So I'll go to jail, so what? We've been in jail for 400 years."

In times of war, the definition of patriotism becomes a matter life or death for Americans and the world. Instead of being feared for our military prowess, we should want to be respected for our dedication to human rights. I suggest that a patriotic American who cares for her or his country might act on behalf of a different vision.

We need to expand the prevailing definition of patriotism beyond that narrow nationalism that has caused so much death and suffering. If national boundaries should not be obstacles to trade—some call it "globalization"—should they also not be obstacles to compassion and generosity?

Should we not begin to consider all children, everywhere, as our own? In that case, war, which in our time is always an assault on children, would be unacceptable as a solution to the problems of the world. Human ingenuity would have to search for other ways.

17

HENRY DAVID THOREAU

In the year 1968 I was called to Milwaukee to testify in the case of the Milwaukee 14, a group of priests, nuns, and laypeople who had gone into a draft board, taken thousands of its documents, and burned them in a symbolic protest against the U.S. war in Vietnam. As a historian of social movements, I was asked to discuss the role of civil disobedience in American history. The judge was clearly uneasy, but he allowed me to answer the question. I spoke of the principles of the Declaration of Independence, and of its insistence that when a government becomes destructive of basic human rights, it is the duty of the people to "alter or abolish it." I began to talk about Henry David Thoreau and his decision to break the law in protest against the U.S. invasion of Mexico in 1846. At this point, Judge Larsen interrupted. He pounded his gavel and said: "You can't discuss that. That is getting to the heart of the matter."

Indeed, Henry David Thoreau's writings get to the heart of the matter. He took on some of the most incendiary issues of his time: the Mexican War, the Fugitive Slave Act, the execution of John Brown. The term "political," however, does not do justice to the breadth and depth of Thoreau's ideas. He looks beyond the immediate subjects of contention to ask the fundamental questions pondered before and after his time by the world's great thinkers: Plato,

Machiavelli, Hobbes, Locke, Rousseau, Marx, Tolstoy. That is, he addresses the obligations of the citizen to government, of law to justice, and of human beings to one another.

The words of Thoreau on all these issues, written more than a century and a half ago, resound today with meaning. The nation is at war, as it was when Thoreau declared his resistance to government. This time, however, it is not a finite war, limited in time and space, but what seems to be an endless war, or series of wars, because the enemy has been declared to be "terrorism," which cannot be confined to one place, or one time. All that Thoreau wrote so long ago speaks to us today and makes us wonder about our responsibility as citizens and human beings.

In fact, Thoreau's work is still incendiary today because he asks the most troubling question of human existence: *how shall we live our lives in a society that makes being human more and more difficult?*

It is well known that Thoreau spent a night in jail during the summer of 1846 because he refused to pay his taxes in protest against the war with Mexico. It may be useful, then, to take a close look at that war, to help us understand his action and his thinking.

Mexico, which had won its independence in a revolutionary war against Spain, was at that time much larger than it is today. It included what are now the states of Texas, New Mexico, Utah, Nevada, Arizona, California, and parts of Wyoming and Colorado. In the year 1836, Texas, aided by the United States, declared its independence from Mexico, calling itself the "Lone Star Republic." It was brought into the Union as a state by act of Congress in 1845, and various influential newspapers and politicians became excited about the prospect of expanding westward into Mexican territory.

The following year, President James Polk, who on the night of his inauguration had confided to his secretary of the navy that he was determined to acquire California, sent troops to the southern border of Texas, as far as the Rio Grande, into territory claimed by Mexico and inhabited by Mexicans. A clash between Mexican and U.S. troops followed, and a U.S. patrol was virtually wiped out. Even before this incident, a U.S. colonel on the southern front, Ethan Allen Hitchcock, a reader of Shakespeare, Chaucer, Hegel, and Spinoza, wrote in his diary: "I have said from the first that the United States are the aggressors. . . . It looks as if the government sent a small force on purpose to bring on war, so as to have a pretext for taking California and as much of this country as it chooses."

President Polk falsely claimed that Mexico had invaded the United States and asked Congress for a declaration of war. The Whig Party was presumably against slavery and against the war, but they were not against expansion, and they saw the acquisition of California as commercially valuable. Thus they voted overwhelmingly with the Democrats in Congress in favor of war. It was an early manifestation of the historic unity of both major parties in acquiescing to a presidential decision for war.

The war against Mexico intensified the bitter controversy already simmering in the United States over slavery. Ralph Waldo Emerson had predicted that "the United States will conquer Mexico, but it will be as the man swallows the arsenic, which brings him down in turn. Mexico will poison us." Commenting on Emerson's warning, the Civil War historian James McPherson has written: "He was right. The poison was slavery." Opposition to the war by the growing antislavery movement was based on the fear that the new

territories would expand the area of slavery in the country.
The poet James Russell Lowell had his character Hosea
Biglow say:

> *They jest want this Californy*
> *So's to lug new slave-states in*
> *To abuse ye, an' to scorn ye,*
> *An' to plunder ye like sin.*

Thoreau lived in Concord, twenty miles from Boston,
which was becoming a center of antislavery agitation. He
graduated from Harvard in 1837. Six years earlier, on
January 3, 1831, William Lloyd Garrison had launched the
first issue of the antislavery newspaper *The Liberator*, declaring of slavery, "On this subject I do not wish to think or
speak or write with moderation. No! No! Tell a man whose
house is on fire to give a moderate alarm."

All about Thoreau there were ardent opponents of slavery, including his mother and sisters. Ralph Waldo Emerson
was a friend and mentor, and the two of them joined forces,
over the objection of conservative curators of the Concord
Lyceum, to invite the fiery abolitionist orator Wendell
Phillips to speak.

In order to protest a government that countenanced slavery, Thoreau refused to pay his poll tax during the six years
prior to the Mexican War. But in the summer of 1846, in the
midst of his two-year stay at Walden Pond to write *A Week
on the Concord and Merrimack Rivers*, and to commune alone
with nature, he ventured into Concord to join a huckleberry-
picking party. There, he encountered the local constable,
who asked him to pay his tax. He refused and was taken to the
town jail. That night, as he lay awake in his cell, the ideas

began to form about how an individual should behave in relation to the government. The next day he was told that someone had appeared to pay his tax (he never found out whether it was his friend Emerson or one of his aunts), and he reluctantly left the jail, to return to the huckleberry field.

The Mexican War ended in 1848 with the United States taking a huge portion of Mexico's land. But before it ended, there were protests against the war going far beyond Thoreau's mild act. The battle deaths and mutilations were not the only horrors of the war. A regimental surgeon of the Second Regiment of Mississippi Rifles saw his regiment packed into the holds of transports and reported on what he saw and heard: "The wild screams of the delirious, the lamentations of the sick, and the melancholy groans of the dying." More than 9,000 soldiers deserted. There were mutinies against officers, resentment against the caste system. One Pennsylvania volunteer wrote: "Some of our officers are very good men but the balance of them are very tyrannical and brutal. . . . A soldier's life is very disgusting."

Thoreau left his cabin at Walden Pond in the fall of 1847. A lecture that he gave soon after at the Concord Lyceum was called "The Rights and Duties of the Individual in Relation to Government." He kept refining it, and it appeared in print in the spring of 1849 as "Resistance to Civil Government." The title "Civil Disobedience" was used in the printing of the essay in 1866, four years after Thoreau's death; the title may or may not have been Thoreau's. Authorial or not, it has become the standard title, the one by which millions have known the essay.

How shall we define civil disobedience so that we may have a common ground for discussing it? I will define it as the deliberate violation of a law in pursuit of some social goal. Thus Thoreau's act of nonpayment of taxes fits that definition, his goal to make some small statement against war, against slavery. Gandhi's marches in violation of British law had as their aim the unseating of British rule in India. The African American students who in 1960 "sat in" at lunch counters to protest racial segregation were violating local law, and even federal law, since the Supreme Court had not given constitutional approval to desegregation in private businesses.

At the center of Thoreau's great essay (though he doesn't make the reference) is that stunning idea expressed in the Declaration of Independence: governments are artificial creations, set up to serve the interests of the people. That idea was quickly overwhelmed by the reality of the Constitution and the establishment of an actual government. Now a small group of powerful men could use the government to advance their own interests, make war, and compromise with slavery. But why should people of conscience defer to such a government and its laws? Why should they not exercise their own moral judgment? When a government supports injustice, it is the duty of its citizens to withhold their support from the government, to resist its demands.

The early 1850s saw a series of militant acts of civil disobedience in violation of the Fugitive Slave Act. There is no evidence of anyone's referring to Thoreau, but clearly the idea of resistance to unjust laws was being put into effect. The passage of the Fugitive Slave Act in 1850 was part of a package of provisions in what was called the Compromise of 1850, designed to satisfy both sides of the slavery dispute. California was admitted to the Union as a non-slave state, but to appease the South, federal marshals were required to help slave owners recapture their escaped slaves and were fined $1,000 if they refused. Federal commissioners were to decide whether in fact a black person was an escaped slave; they were paid ten dollars if they decided in favor of the slave owner, five dollars if they decided in favor of the slave. During that decade of the 1850s, federal commissioners returned 332 blacks to slavery and declared only 11 free. There was no statute of limitations: one black man in southern Indiana was apprehended, in front of his wife and children, and returned to a slaveholder who said the man had run away nineteen years before.

Almost as soon as the act went into effect and the first escaped slaves were apprehended, Northern abolitionists, black and white, set out to obstruct the law. A slave owner in Georgia sent two agents to recapture William and Ellen Craft, a husband and wife who had escaped slavery two years earlier and were now living in Boston, a center of abolitionism. Blacks and whites joined to protect the Crafts. Wendell Phillips declared: "We must trample this law under our feet." The law, said the local antislavery society, "is to be denounced, resisted, and disobeyed." The slave catchers were warned that they were not safe in Boston, and they returned to Georgia. William and Ellen Craft were put on a ship to England.

President Millard Fillmore threatened to send federal troops to enforce the Fugitive Slave Act, but the abolitionists defied him. The Reverend Theodore Parker, an abolitionist whose parish the Crafts had joined, wrote to Fillmore: "I would rather lie all my life in jail, and starve there, than refuse to protect one of these parishioners of mine . . . I must reverence the laws of God, come of that what will come."

There were more acts of defiance against the Fugitive

Slave Act. Shadrach Minkins, a black man who had escaped from Virginia and was working as a waiter in a Boston coffeehouse, was captured by agents and taken to a federal courthouse. A group of men broke into the courtroom, rescued Minkins, and put him on the Underground Railroad to Canada. Eight of the rescuers, four black and four white, were indicted by a federal grand jury. But when they went to trial, juries refused to convict them.

In Christiana, Pennsylvania, a shoot-out took place over the attempt of a slave owner and federal marshals to return two black men to slavery. Two dozen black men protected the fugitives, and the slave owner was killed. President Fillmore called on the marines, who, with federal marshals, searched the countryside and arrested more than thirty black men and a half-dozen whites. They were indicted, but the jury acquitted the first defendant and the government dropped the remaining cases.

Thoreau's essay, "Slavery in Massachusetts," was drawn from journal entries of 1851 and 1854, and appeared in part in Garrison's *The Liberator.* That essay has been overshadowed by his more famous one on civil disobedience, but it deserves close attention. He was provoked by an incident in 1854, when President Franklin Pierce dispatched federal troops, joined by state militia and local police, to capture Anthony Burns, a slave escaped from Virginia. Black and white abolitionists used a battering ram against the courthouse doors but they were repulsed. Burns was marched to the waterfront, through streets lined with his supporters, to the sound of church bells tolling, and sent back to slavery.

In his essay, Thoreau touches on the complicity of the government and the courts, the silence of citizens in the face of that collusion ("I am surprised to see men going about their business as if nothing had happened"), and the cowardice of the press. Thoreau does not expect the government to act in the interests of justice and believes that in the long run this will be widely recognized: "A government which deliberately enacts injustice, and persists in it, will at length ever become the laughing-stock of the world." One cannot help recalling that the United States drew the opposition of people all over the world when it made war with Vietnam in the 1960s, and that 10 million people in fifty countries around the world protested on a single day when the United States was on the verge of invading Iraq in 2003,

Thoreau did not have much hope for the government ("useless, or worse than useless") nor for the soldier who serves the slave master ("a fool made conspicuous by a painted coat"). But he expected more from citizens and so was bitter about their silence when a fugitive slave, Thomas Sims, was forcibly returned to slavery in 1851. He noted that the people of Concord—on the anniversary of the shot heard round the world in 1775, and just a week after the rendition of Sims—rang the liberty bells and fired the cannons. But "when the sound of the bells died away, their liberty died away also." That could be a commentary on any celebration in the midst of war.

Thoreau has no respect for the law when the law allows war and protects slaveholders, nor does he have respect for the justices of the Supreme Court, as they, obedient to the Constitution, affirm the legality of holding 3 million people as slaves. "The law will never make men free; it is men who have got to make the law free." Such judges do not ask what the murderers' tools are for; they only inspect them to see whether they are "in working order." Such judges do not ask "whether the Fugitive Slave Law is right, but whether it is what they call *constitutional.*" In "Slavery in Massachusetts," Thoreau writes: "What is wanted is men, not of policy, but of probity—who recognize a higher law than the Constitution, or the decision of the majority." Thoreau's attitude toward law and toward the Constitution points very directly to the legal controversies of our own time, when certain Supreme Court justices and legal scholars insist their job is to decide what the Founding Fathers meant by the words they wrote in 1787. Thoreau asks why, in deciding moral questions, we must ask whether "your grandfather, seventy years ago" entered into an agreement "to serve the devil" and therefore you must abide by that agreement, regardless of its human consequences.

Thoreau could have been speaking about Justice Abe Fortas, who joined the Supreme Court majority in the spring of 1968 to uphold the conviction of a young man who had publicly burned his draft card to protest the war in Vietnam (a petty act of arson, one might say, compared with William Lloyd Garrison's setting fire to the Constitution in 1835). The court was not concerned with whether the war was right (or even whether it was constitutional) but considered only whether O'Brien had violated the Conscription Act.

That same year, in an essay on civil disobedience, Fortas wrote: "Thoreau was an inspiring figure and a great writer; but his essay should not be read as a handbook on political science." His notion of "political science" clearly did not include moral philosophy but made the former a register of whatever regulations the politicians of the time might order.

In "Slavery in Massachusetts," Thoreau is scathing about the press. The newspaper, he said, "is a Bible which we read every morning and every afternoon, standing and sitting, riding and walking." Editors, he said, by their acceptance of the Fugitive Slave Act, "live and rule only by their own servility." Speaking of a certain Boston newspaper and its response when Thomas Sims was carried off to slavery, he wrote: "I have heard the gurgling of the sewer through every column." What would Thoreau say if he were alive today? In our time, too, the press (much of it controlled by huge financial conglomerates) is largely subservient to government, especially in time of war, when a fervid nationalism distorts reportage and criticism of government policy is often seen as unpatriotic. According to Daniel Hallin's careful study, The "Uncensored War": The Media and Vietnam, television coverage throughout the Vietnam War was "lopsidedly favorable to American policy in Vietnam," even more so than what he called the "remarkably docile print media."

In the current Iraq War, the major television channels rushed to declare their support for U.S. aggression. The Fox News Channel regularly showed the Stars and Stripes in the upper-left-hand corner of the screen, and the words "War on terror" blended into "Operation Iraqi Freedom." According to a study by Fairness and Accuracy in Reporting, even though at the moment that Bush declared "Mission Accomplished" in Iraq 27 percent of the public remained opposed to the war, of those people chosen by the major television networks to be interviewed, less than 3 percent were antiwar.

What Thoreau saw as a coldness from the government and the press toward the black slave, an abysmal failure of compassion for the "other," persisted for a hundred years, even after the end of slavery, in the continued subordination of black people in this country. To white Americans, black people were a shadowy presence, unknown as full human beings.

Thoreau saw the national and local governments of his time collaborating with slavery. Until the 1960s, we saw the national government acquiescing in racial segregation in violation of the Fourteenth and Fifteenth Amendments. Only when black people in the South pushed themselves into view and brought public attention by acts of civil disobedience, did government finally respond.

The invisibility of the "other" carries over into war, where the "enemy" is other than human and need not be considered when the casualties start mounting up. Nowhere was this revealed more starkly than when atomic bombs destroyed Hiroshima and Nagasaki. The incineration and radiation of several hundred thousand Japanese could be accepted by Americans because they were not seen as human beings, not made visible as were the victims of Japan in the Bataan Death March or, some time after the fact, the victims of Hitler in the death camps.

Similarly, the Vietnamese who died or were maimed or burned by napalm in the ferocious bombing of their country (more bombs were dropped there than in all of World War II) were not visible to Americans for many years. Their deaths were recorded as statistics, but they did not appear as human beings until the first photos of the My Lai Massacre appeared a year after it was first reported in 1968.

Such callousness would have troubled Thoreau deeply. "I would remind my countrymen, that they are to be men first, and Americans only at a late and convenient hour." Civil disobedience is inherently antinationalist because it is based on a refusal to accept the legitimacy of government as an absolute; it considers the powers of government subordinate to human rights. The implication is that these rights belong to all human beings, not just those of one's own country. Black slaves were not quite of the United States. Indeed, they had been denied citizenship by the decision of the Supreme Court in the *Dred Scott* case of 1857. Yet Thoreau declared their rights to be above the law of the nation, even above the highest law of the nation—the Constitution.

Thoreau's essay propounded such a universal principle of human rights that it continues to be an inspiration for dissident thinkers and activists around the world. Tolstoy took note of "the savage Spanish-American war" and wrote of a "second war" waged against the government, its powerful weapon being "the obedience of every man to his own reason and conscience." Tolstoy wrote:

> This, indeed, is so simple, so indubitable, and binding upon every man. "You wish to make me a participator in murder; you demand of me money for the preparation of weapons; and want me to take part in the organized assembly of murderers" says the reasonable man—he who had neither sold nor obscured his conscience. "But I profess that law—the same that is also professed by you—which long ago forbade not murder only, but all hostility, also, and therefore I cannot obey you."

Gandhi knew of both Thoreau and Tolstoy. Thoreau, he wrote, "has left a masterly treatise on the Duty of Civil Disobedience." The influence can be seen in the campaigns Gandhi organized to protest British rule in India. In 1919 the British passed the Rowlatt Act (remarkably similar to the USA PATRIOT Act passed by Congress in 2001) that provided for preventive detention, the arrest and confinement of

persons who were "suspected of subversive activities."
Persons considered "dangerous" could be detained indefinitely. Gandhi and his followers took a pledge: "We solemnly
affirm that . . . we shall refuse civilly to obey these laws." In
1930 Gandhi and others participated in a civil disobedience
movement against the government monopoly on salt and the
oppressive salt tax. They marched from Ahmadabad to the
beach at Dandi and prepared salt from the sea, thus violating the salt laws. Gandhi was arrested, but the civil disobedience continued for a year, in the course of which salt
depots were occupied, and protesters were met with brutal
police attacks.

In the United States social movements throughout the
twentieth century and into the twenty-first repeatedly put
moral principles ahead of the law. Thoreau had written,
"Must the citizen ever for a moment, or in the least degree,
resign his conscience to the legislator? Why has every man
a conscience, then? . . . It is not desirable to cultivate a
respect for the law, so much as for the right."

In this spirit, labor organizers in the Industrial Workers
of the World went to jail again and again in defiance of local
laws. On the eve of World War I, women picketed in the
nation's capital in violation of local ordinances and were
arrested for demanding the right to vote. In 1936 and 1937,
workers in auto and rubber plants staged sit-down strikes
to get recognition for their unions.

In the 1950s and 1960s, black people in the South carried out hundreds of acts of civil disobedience, refusing to
obey the laws mandating racial segregation, defying the laws
of trespass, disobeying orders of police. Thoreau had written: "I quietly declare war with the State, after my fashion."
Black people in the South had concluded that the U.S. gov-

ernment would not defend their constitutional rights under the Fourteenth and Fifteenth Amendments, and they would take action themselves.

A white city librarian in Montgomery, Alabama, wrote a letter to the *Montgomery Advertiser*, saying admiringly that the black people boycotting the city buses that winter of 1955 "had taken a lesson from Gandhi, and from our own Thoreau, who influenced Gandhi." The young seminary student John Lewis, who was beaten senseless in the attempted protest march in 1965 from Selma to Montgomery, had studied Gandhi and Thoreau.

No one energized the idea of civil disobedience in the United States more than Martin Luther King Jr. He was a student of philosophy and religion and was very aware of Thoreau and Gandhi; no doubt their powerful ideas reinforced his own thinking. But it was the reality of racial segregation that led him and the thousands of others in the Southern movement—the sit-inners, the Freedom Riders, the marchers, and picketers—to defy the law again and again.

In King's famous "Letter from Birmingham City Jail," he distinguishes between "just and unjust laws" in the way that Thoreau had distinguished between taxes he was willing to pay because they went for constructive public purposes and taxes he would not pay because they supported a government at war. King had been arrested for violating a court injunction against demonstrations. "An unjust law," he said, "is out of harmony with the moral law."

The practice of civil disobedience was carried over from the protests against racial segregation to the movement against the war in Vietnam. Indeed, among the first to resist the draft (and to receive especially heavy prison sentences) were young black men in the South. In mid-1965, as the war in Vietnam began escalating rapidly, blacks in McComb, Mississippi, who had just learned that a classmate had been killed in Vietnam, distributed a leaflet: "No Mississippi Negroes should be fighting in Vietnam for the White man's freedom, until all the Negro People are free in Mississippi. Negro boys should not honor the draft here in Mississippi. Mothers should encourage their sons not to go." Among the most dramatic instances of civil disobedience against the war was that of heavyweight champion Muhammad Ali, who refused to serve in what he called a "white man's war." As punishment, boxing authorities took away his title as champion.

At no time in American history was there such a succession of acts of civil disobedience as during the war in Vietnam. Young men burned their draft cards or turned them in to the government. They refused to be inducted into the armed forces, 34,000 of them by the end of 1969. Hundreds of thousands, without going public in their refusal, did not register for the draft.

Americans were deeply offended by these actions and argued that citizens should express themselves by going through legal channels like voting. But Thoreau had no faith that government officials would act morally: "most legislators, politicians, lawyers, ministers, and office-holders, serve the State chiefly with their heads; and, as they rarely make any moral distinctions, they are as likely to serve the devil, without intending it, as God." He was disdainful of voting and other orthodox remedies. "They take too much time, and a man's life will be gone."

That spirit animated the priests, nuns, and laypeople who throughout the war in Vietnam broke into draft boards, seized draft records, and destroyed them to dramatize their protest against the war. During the trial of the Milwaukee

14, a priest named Bob Cunnane told the court that he had tried to go through legal channels to help stop the war, that he had visited his senator and was told that people in Congress were helpless. For this reason he decided on an action more forceful, even if it meant breaking the law and going to prison.

Disobedience spread to the armed forces. Early in the war, one West Point graduate refused to board an aircraft that would take him to a remote Vietnamese village. Three army privates refused to embark for Vietnam, denouncing the war as "immoral, illegal, and unjust"; they were court-martialed and imprisoned. An army doctor refused to teach Green Berets, a Special Forces elite, saying they were "murderers of women and children."

Tens of thousands deserted from the military, going to Canada or to Western Europe. B-52 pilots refused to go on missions during the fierce bombings of Hanoi and Haiphong in December 1972. Earlier that year, 50 out of 142 GIs in one company refused to go out on patrol.

After the war in Vietnam ended in 1975, a determined group of pacifists continued to protest the militarization of our country, the buildup of nuclear weapons, by acts of civil disobedience. Beginning in 1980 with a group called the Plowshares Eight (taking their name from the biblical injunction to beat swords into plowshares), they invaded nuclear facilities, committing small symbolic acts of sabotage. In the next twenty-three years at least seventy-five similar actions were carried out, almost always resulting in jail sentences.

Although it was supported by most Americans, the First Gulf War in 1990–91 led to mass demonstrations of protest in American cities, as well as to refusals of military service by young men and women. A physician named Lynda Reiser, explaining why she would defy the order sending her to Iraq, wrote: "I object to participation in war in any form. I believe in the preservation of life at all costs. . . . I cannot participate in war, either as a combatant or as a non-combatant, because my doing so would represent my agreement with war."

This is exactly what Thoreau advocated in the face of evils like slavery and war: that people should withdraw their support from the government. It is not enough to hold an opinion, he said. One must act. "When the subject has refused allegiance, and the officer has resigned his office, then the revolution is accomplished."

Thoreau's next sentences are disquieting and make it clear he was not an absolute pacifist. "But even suppose blood should flow. Is there not a sort of blood shed when the conscience is wounded?" He seems to have accepted that an evil as gross as slavery—the captivity of 3 million people—could not be overcome without some degree of violence.

John Brown's life epitomized the belief that violence would be necessary to abolish slavery. With a small band of like-minded men, he went to Kansas, which had become a battleground between proslavery and antislavery forces. There were killings on both sides, and at one point Brown and his men carried out a nighttime raid on a proslavery settlement and killed five people in cold blood.

Thoreau delivered to the citizens of Concord his lecture "A Plea for Captain John Brown" twelve days after Brown, with his sons and a small group of white and black abolitionists, tried to seize the federal arsenal at Harpers Ferry, Virginia. Their aim was to incite a general slave revolt, but the plan miscarried, they were captured, and Brown lay wounded, awaiting trial.

Thoreau's passionate talk is not a defense of John Brown but, as he titled it, a plea, an expression of sympathy and admiration. It is very unlikely that Thoreau would have participated in the kind of action Brown had engaged in, yet he defended Brown's "right to interfere by force with the slaveholder, in order to rescue the slave." Brown's firearms, he said, "were employed in a righteous cause."

Emerson, with a similar passion, said of John Brown that "he will make the gallows glorious like the cross." Emerson and Thoreau were both outraged at the rush by both the state of Virginia and the national government to execute Brown, and the "cold-blooded way," as Thoreau put it, that newspaper editors and others, even abolitionists, talked of the man as "dangerous" and "insane." Shortly after John Brown was hanged for killing people, believing he was advancing the cause of freedom for slaves, the U.S. government engaged in a war, presumably to abolish slavery, and 600,000 died on the battlefields. Would any one dare to refer to the U.S. government as "dangerous" and "insane"?

Running through Thoreau's essay about John Brown is a powerful theme that speaks to our own time: the hypocrisy of government officials who, with an air of righteousness, buttressed by the law, put to death killers of one, two, or ten persons, but who themselves plan and carry out wars in which millions die.

"War is peace" was the slogan of the Big Brother state described in George Orwell's novel 1984. We carry out wars in the name of peace. In the United States we keep 2 million people in prison in the name of order. Thoreau's words speak directly to our time: "We preserve the so-called 'peace' of our community by deeds of petty violence every day. Look at the policeman's billy and hand cuffs! Look at the jail! Look at the gallows!'"

We are speaking not of totalitarian governments but of governments that call themselves democracies as does ours. We pride ourselves on having representative government. But, as Thoreau says, still speaking of John Brown, "what a monster of a government is that where the noblest faculties of the mind, and the *whole* heart, are not *represented*."

Thoreau's great insight is that there is a moral emptiness in government unless it is filled by the actions of citizens on behalf of justice. That corresponds exactly to the democratic philosophy of the Declaration of Independence, in which governments have no inherent right to exist or to rule, but deserve to do so only when they fulfill the charge given them by the people: to protect everyone's equal right to "life, liberty, and the pursuit of happiness."

In our time, that philosophy is realized in the actions of those who, in defiance of government, in defiance of laws they consider supportive of war and injustice, carry out acts of civil disobedience. That might mean damaging weapons of war or refusing to pay taxes to support a huge military budget or refusing to join a military campaign seen as destructive of human life. In the end, behind the hard actions of civil disobedience (soft in relation to the actions of government), there is a desire for a life in which all that will be unnecessary. Thoreau's essay "Life without Principle," published posthumously in 1963 in the *Atlantic Monthly*, expresses ideas developed through a number of lectures he gave between 1854 and 1860. Thoreau's final working title for the piece was "The Higher Law," which today provides fresh insight into our very modern lives.

In "Life without Principle," Thoreau joins his criticism of government and society with his love of the natural world. *How shall we live?* he asks. "This world is a place of business." Money rules our lives but does not enrich them. "The ways by which you may get money almost without exception lead downward."

Are Thoreau's ideas utopian, and therefore useless, in a world of technological marvels, global commerce, and powerful nations? Or is it perhaps that Thoreau is asking that technology be tamed to serve our existential needs for peace and beauty, that commerce serve not greed, but human life, that nations be communities and not war machines? He is not against the "things" of modern life but wants to change the situation that Emerson described: "Things are in the saddle and ride mankind."

In the midst of the struggle for justice, however, Thoreau is convinced that right will prevail. Agitated as he is about the evil of slavery—"Who can be serene in a country where both the rulers and the ruled are without principle?"—he is brought back to himself when he scents a white water-lily and realizes that a season he "had waited for had arrived." The lily "suggests what kind of laws have prevailed longest and widest, and still prevail, and that the time may come when man's deeds will smell as sweet."

18

NATIONALISM

During recent coverage of the national debate on immigration I saw something deeply disturbing: news photos of ordinary Americans sitting on chairs, guns on their laps, standing unofficial guard on the Arizona border to make sure no undocumented Mexicans cross over into the United States. There was something horrifying in the realization that, in this twenty-first century of what we call "civilization," we have carved up the world into 200 artificially created entities we call "nations" and have armed ourselves to arrest or attack anyone who crosses a boundary.

Is not nationalism—that devotion to a flag, an anthem, a boundary, so fierce it engenders mass murder—one of the great evils of our time, along with racism and religious hatred? These ways of thinking—cultivated, nurtured, indoctrinated from childhood on—have been useful to those in power, and deadly for those "others" outside the dominating ethnic, racial, or religious groups.

National spirit can be benign in a small country that is lacking military power and a hunger for expansion (Switzerland, Norway, Costa Rica, and many more). But in a nation like ours—huge, possessing thousands of weapons of mass destruction—what might have been harmless pride becomes an arrogant nationalism dangerous to others and to ourselves.

Our citizenry has been brought up to see our nation as different from others, an exception in the world, uniquely moral, expanding into other lands in order to bring civilization, liberty, and democracy.

That self-deception started early. When the first English settlers moved into American Indian land in Massachusetts Bay and were resisted, the violence escalated into war with the Pequot Indians. The killing of American Indians was seen as approved by God, the taking of land as commanded by the Bible. The Puritans cited one of the Psalms, which says: "Ask of me, and I shall give thee, the heathen for thine inheritance, and the uttermost parts of the Earth for thy possession."

On the eve of the Mexican War, John O'Sullivan, editor of the *Democratic Review*, wrote that it was the nation's "manifest destiny to overspread the continent allotted by Providence for the free development of our yearly multiplying millions." The phrase took hold: Manifest Destiny. After the invasion of Mexico began, the *New York Herald* announced: "We believe it is a part of our destiny to civilize that beautiful country."

Nationalism is given a special virulence when it is blessed by Providence. At the beginning of the twentieth century, when the United States invaded the Philippines, President McKinley said that the decision to take the Philippines came one night when he got down on his knees and prayed and God told him to take the country. As our armies were committing massacres in the Philippines, Elihu Root, our Secretary of War, was saying "The American soldier is different from all other soldiers of all other countries since the war began. He is the advance guard of liberty and justice, of law and order, and of peace and happiness."

Our culture is permeated by a Christian fundamentalism as poisonous as that of Cotton Mather. It permits the mass murder of "the other" with the same confidence as it accepts the death penalty for individuals convicted of crimes. Speaking of capital punishment, Supreme Court Justice Antonin Scalia told an audience at the University of Chicago Divinity School: "For the believing Christian, death is no big deal."

Today we have a president, currently at war in two countries, who believes he gets messages from God. For an article in the Israeli newspaper *Ha'aretz*, a reporter talked with Palestinian leaders who had met with President Bush. One of them reported that Bush said to him: "God told me to strike at Al Qaeda, and I struck them, and then he instructed me to strike at Saddam, which I did, and now I am determined to solve the problem in the Middle East." It's hard to know if the quote is authentic, especially because it is so literate. But it certainly is consistent with Bush's oft-expressed claims.

Years before that, in 1993, President Bill Clinton, speaking at a West Point commencement, declared: "The values you learned here . . . will be able to spread throughout this country and throughout the world and give other people the opportunity to live as you have lived, to fulfill your God-given capacities."

Not every U.S. leader has claimed divine sanction, but the idea has persisted that the United States is uniquely justified in using its power to expand throughout the world. In 1945, at the end of World War II, Henry Luce, the owner of a vast chain of media enterprises—*Time, LIFE, Fortune*—declared that this would be "the American Century," that victory in the war gave the United States the right "to exert upon the world the full impact of our influence, for such purposes as we see fit and by such means as we see fit."

This confident prophecy has been acted out through the rest of the twentieth century up to the present day. Almost immediately after World War II, the United States penetrated the oil regions of the Middle East by special arrangements with Saudi Arabia. It established military bases in Japan, Korea, the Philippines, and a number of Pacific islands. In the next decades it orchestrated right-wing coups in Iran, Guatemala, and Chile, and gave military aid to various dictatorships in the Caribbean. It soon had military bases all over the world, and in an attempt to establish a foothold in Southeast Asia, it invaded Vietnam and bombed Laos and Cambodia.

The reasons given to the public and to the world have varied in their specifics, but common to all of the explanations has been the claim of moral purpose: promoting democracy; stopping the spread of communism; preserving liberty; saving lives; eliminating weapons of mass destruction.

The real reasons lie elsewhere: in the urge to plant American power in more and more parts of the globe; in the need to control vital resources in the interests of corporate profit; in the political ambitions of presidents; in the usefulness of foreign adventures to divert attention from domestic problems.

But it should be noted that where American policy could not be justified in the name of democracy—because it involved overthrowing democratically elected governments—the military intervention was carried out in secret through what a Senate Committee in 1975 called "covert action."

Thus, in Chile, in 1973, the government of Salvador Allende, which had been democratically elected, was overthrown by a military coup supported by the United States.

There was no need to explain this to the American public in moral terms because the public did not know. It was a secret operation of the Nixon administration, with Henry Kissinger in charge, working with officials of the International Telephone and Telegraph Corporation, which had important interests in Chile.

According to the report of the Senate Committee headed by Frank Church, in its special section titled "Covert Action in Chile," "In 1970, the U.S. government and several multinational corporations were linked in opposition to the candidacy and later the presidency of Salvador Allende."

The overthrow of Allende was followed by a military dictatorship in Chile, under General Pinochet, in which thousands of Chileans were murdered, thousands others tortured, and thousands disappeared. Behind the scenes, Kissinger was assuring Pinochet: "In the United States, as you know, we are sympathetic with what you are trying to do here. . . . We wish your government well."

In other cases, where the military intervention was overt, the public had to be given reasons. Thus, during the presidency of Ronald Reagan, in October of 1983, United States military forces occupied the tiny Caribbean island of Grenada, where a left-wing government was in power. The excuses were that American medical students in Grenada were in danger (shown later not to be true), and that Grenada was a possible future base for either Cuba or the Soviet Union (a wild exaggeration). It was an opportunity to add another piece to the American sphere of influence in the Caribbean.

In the first year of his presidency, George H. W. Bush's (Bush, the father) ordered American forces to invade Panama. The reason given was to stop drug trafficking by deposing the dictatorial ruler of Panama, Manuel Noriega. In fact, Noriega had once worked for the Central Intelligence Agency (CIA) and was supported by the United States. But by 1989 his usefulness was over; he was no longer considered a friend, and the United States wanted a government in Panama that would be more compliant to U.S. interests. The invasion cost very few American lives, but hundreds, perhaps thousands of Panamanian lives. Neighborhoods in Panama City were ruthlessly bombed.

Noriega was captured, brought to trial, found guilty, and sent to prison. A new president friendly to the United States was installed in Panama, but poverty and unemployment persisted, and in 1992 the *New York Times* reported that the invasion and removal of Noriega "failed to stanch the flow of illicit narcotics through Panama."

The United States did succeed in what can be considered an imperial ambition: to reestablish dominance over Panama. The *New York Times* reported: "The President [of Panama] and his key aides and the American Ambassador, Deane Hinton, have breakfast together once a week in a meeting that many Panamanians view as the place where important decisions are taken."

But the Panama operation was on too small a scale to accomplish what the Reagan and Bush administrations badly wanted: to overcome the American public's abhorrence, since Vietnam, of foreign military interventions.

Two years later, the First Gulf War against Iraq presented such an opportunity. Iraq, under the brutal dictatorship of Saddam Hussein, had taken over its small but oil-rich neighbor, Kuwait, in August of 1990. This provided an ideal excuse for military intervention. And Bush needed a foreign adventure to boost his popularity. On October 16, 1990, the

Washington Post had a front-page story headline: "Poll Shows Plunge in Public Confidence. Bush's Rating Plummets." The same newspaper reported later the same month: "Some observers in his own party worry that the president will be forced to initiate combat to prevent further erosion of his support at home."

After the November 1990 elections brought gains for the Democrats in Congress, Bush doubled American military forces in the Gulf to 500,000. The journalist Elizabeth Drew reported that Bush's Chief of Staff John Sununu "was telling people that a short successful war would be pure political gold for the President and would guarantee his election."

The American public was told that the motivation for armed intervention was to liberate Kuwait from Iraqi control, but the United States, ever since the end of World War II, had determined to make itself the major power in the control of Middle East oil. Shortly after the brief 1991 war in Iraq, representatives of the thirteen oil-producing nations were about to gather in Geneva, and the business correspondent of the *New York Times* wrote: "By virtue of its military victory the United States is likely to have more influence in the Organization of Petroleum Exporting Countries than any industrial nation has ever exercised."

In mid-January of 1991, the United States launched its war against Iraq, giving it the name "Operation Desert Storm." The government and the media had conjured up a picture of a formidable military power, but Iraq was hardly that. The war was over in six weeks. But it involved ferocious bombing and the killing of untold numbers of civilians.

The American invasion did not push to Baghdad. Saddam Hussein was deliberately left in power, and dissident

Kurds and Shiites, who had been promised support, were abandoned. A *New York Times* dispatch reported: "President Bush has decided to let President Saddam Hussein put down rebellions in his country without American intervention rather than risk the splintering of Iraq, according to official statements and private briefings today."

The man who had been Jimmy Carter's National Security Adviser, Zbigniew Brzezinski, summed up the venture with a nod to a moral crusade and an explicit recognition of the imperial objective: "The benefits are undeniably impressive. First, a blatant act of aggression was rebuffed and punished. . . . Second, U.S. military power is henceforth likely to be taken more seriously. . . . Third, the Middle East and Persian Gulf region is now clearly an American sphere of preponderance."

The events of 9/11 intensified nationalist superpatriotism and gave the Bush administration immediate rationale to attack Afghanistan. It also enabled Bush to begin threatening North Korea, Iran, and Iraq as being parts of an "Axis of Evil." There was reason to doubt that deploying American forces to Afghanistan was entirely intended to end terrorism. The United States government itself noted that there were terrorist cells in tweny or thirty other countries in the world. Indeed, after five years of bombing and military operations there, the threat of terrorism is as strong as ever. The notoriously evil Taliban regime in Afghanistan was overthrown, but to this day the Taliban movement continues to regroup and combat U.S. forces. The new regime in Afghanistan, with a president hastily installed by the United States, is hardly a democracy, and the plight of women, though improved, remains desperate.

What seems clear is that as a result of operations in

Afghanistan, the United States gained new military bases not only in Afghanistan itself, but in the former Soviet republics of Central Asia as well.

An Associated Press dispatch of January 15, 2002, by Sally Buzbee reported: "Even before September 11, the military had a presence in 140 countries worldwide. Now it is busy expanding—or considering expansion—not just in Afghanistan . . . and neighboring Uzbekistan and Kyrgyzstan, but in a slew of countries beyond: Armenia and Azerbaijan in Central Asia to Somali in East Africa, to the Philippines and Indonesia in Southeast Asia."

There is much evidence that the oil reserves of the Caspian Sea area were an important consideration in the establishment of American control in Afghanistan. A few days before September 11, 2001, the U.S. Energy Information Administration documented Afghanistan's strategic "geographical position as a potential transit route for oil and natural gas exports from Central Asia to the Caspian Sea."

After a year of bombing Afghanistan, the United States suddenly turned its attention to Iraq and began to prepare for war. Its rationale was that Iraq had "weapons of mass destruction" and insisted, on the basis of a UN resolution, that a UN inspection team should investigate.

The UN inspectors reported that there was no evidence of development of a single nuclear weapon, and could not find evidence of chemical and biological weapons, but the United States insisted they must exist. It sent over 200,000 troops into the Middle East, and enough planes and ships to launch a full-scale invasion, and prepared (as this is being written in March, 2003) to bomb and subdue Iraq.

The various reasons given by the Bush administration for

making war on Iraq were so unpersuasive that other members of the UN Security Council, normally supportive of American policy, wouldn't give their agreement. Public opinion all over the world was overwhelmingly against a United States attack. On February 15, 2003, 10 to 12 million people in sixty different countries took to the streets to protest against the impending war. This in itself suggested that the Bush claim that Iraq was a threat to the world had no substance.

Clearly, the American aim had nothing to do with the existence of Iraqi weapons. Many other nations had far greater arsenals; there were at least eight countries in the world possessing nuclear weapons and Iraq had none. That the United States wanted to rid Iraq of its tyrant and establish democracy seemed an empty claim considering the American record of supporting tyrannies all around the globe.

Indeed, the imperial aim of controlling Iraqi's huge oil reserves and establishing a military presence in Iraq was so clear that even liberal commentators in the United States acknowledged it, but claimed the imperialism would be benign.

Michael Ignatieff, a Harvard professor, wrote in the *New York Times*: "America's empire is not like empires of times past, built on colonies, conquest and the white man's burden. We are no longer in the era of the United Fruit Company, when American corporations needed the Marines to secure their investments overseas. The twenty-first century imperium is a new invention in the annals of political science, an empire lite, a global hegemony whose grace notes are free markets, human rights, and democracy."

Only someone blind to the history of the United States,

its obsessive drive for control of oil, its endless expansion of military bases around the world, its domination of other countries through its enormous economic power, its violations of human rights for millions of people, whether directly or through proxy governments, could make that statement.

Nationalist superpatriotism has by no means been confined to Republicans. When Richard Hofstadter analyzed American presidents in his book *The American Political Tradition*, he found that Democratic leaders as well as Republicans, liberals as well as conservatives, invaded other countries and sought to expand U.S. power across the globe.

Liberal imperialists, in fact, have been among the most fervent expansionists, more effective in their claim to moral rectitude precisely because they are liberal on issues other than foreign policy. Theodore Roosevelt, a lover of war, and an enthusiastic supporter of the war against Spain and the conquest of the Philippines, is still seen as a Progressive because he supported certain domestic reforms and was concerned with the natural environment. Indeed, he ran for president on the Progressive ticket in 1912.

Woodrow Wilson, a Democrat, was the epitome of the liberal apologist for violent actions abroad. In April of 1914, he ordered the bombardment of the Mexican coast and the occupation of the city of Veracruz, in retaliation for the Mexican arrest of several U.S. sailors. He sent U.S. Marines into Haiti in 1915, killing thousands of Haitians who resisted, beginning a long military occupation of that tiny country. He sent U.S. Marines to occupy the Dominican Republic in 1916. And, after running in 1916 on a platform of peace, he brought the nation into the slaughter that was taking place in Europe in World War I, saying it was a war to "make the world safe for democracy."

One of the effects of nationalist thinking is a loss of a sense of proportion. The killing of 2,300 people at Pearl Harbor becomes the justification for killing 240,000 in Hiroshima and Nagasaki. The killing of 3,000 people on September 11, 2001, becomes the justification for killing tens of thousands of people in Afghanistan and Iraq and the indefinite detention of hundreds of people at U.S. prison camps at Guantánamo Bay, Cuba, and at secret U.S. facilities around the globe.

What makes our nation immune from the normal standards of human decency?

Surely, we must renounce nationalism and all its symbols: its flags, its pledges of allegiance, its anthems, its insistence in song that God must single out America to be blessed.

We need to assert our allegiance to humanity as a whole, to all living things, and not to any one nation. We need to refute the idea that our nation is different from, morally superior to, the other imperial powers of world history.

Poets and artists—from Euripides to Bob Dylan—seem to have a clearer understanding of the limits of nationalism and its consequence: war. In 1935, Jean Giraudoux, the French playwright, with the memory of the First World War still in his head, wrote *The Trojan War Will Not Take Place*. Demokos, a Trojan soldier, asks the aged Hecuba to tell him "what war looks like." She responds: "Like the backside of a baboon. When the baboon is up in a tree, with its hind end facing us, there is the face of war exactly: scarlet, scaly, glazed, framed in a clotted, filthy wig."

Langston Hughes (no wonder he was called before the House Committee on Un-American Activities) addressed his country as follows:

You really haven't been a virgin for so long
It's ludicrous to keep up the pretext . . .
You've slept with all the big powers
In military uniforms
And you've taken the sweet life
Of all the little brown fellows . . .
Being one of the world's big vampires
Why don't you come out and say so
Like Japan, and England, and France
And all the other nymphomaniacs of power.

Henry David Thoreau, provoked by the war in Mexico and the nationalist fervor it produced, wrote: "Nations! What are nations? . . . Like insects, they swarm. The historian strives in vain to make them memorable." In our time, Kurt Vonnegut's *Cat's Cradle* places nations among those unnatural abstractions he calls "granfalloons," which he defines as "a proud and meaningless association of human beings."

There have always been women and men in this country who have insisted that universal standards of decent human conduct apply to our nation as to others. That insistence continues today and reaches out to people all over the world. It lets them know, like the balloons sent over the countryside by the Paris Commune in 1871, that "our interests are the same."

19

LAND MINES

On August 3, 2005, Human Rights Watch announced that the Bush administration was "poised to resume the production of anti-personnel mines" for the first time since 1997. It noted that "the Pentagon has requested a total of $1.3 billion" for a new type of land mine.

This registered with me because I had just read Dr. Gino Strada's *Green Parrots: A War Surgeon's Diary*. The book tells of his fifteen years performing surgery in Afghanistan, Iraq, Bosnia, Somalia, Eritrea, Cambodia, and other places, on victims of land mines and other products of our technological expertise. The "green parrots" are land mines with tiny wings. Children pick them—with horrible consequences—because the mines look like winged toys.

Strada writes:

> The countries, the names, the skin colors change, but the story of these wretched ones is tragically similar. There is the one who is walking in the meadow, the one who is playing in the backyard or who is shepherding goats, the one who tills the ground or who gathers its fruits. Then the blast. . . . Djamila felt a metallic click under her foot and had a fraction of a second to think before her left leg disintegrated. . . . Many others like Esfandyar do not

remember a thing. A deafening noise and they are hurled on the ground. . . . They wrapped Esfandyar in a big sheet, and they loaded him in the back of a farm truck. Esfandyar did not complain—the father told us—not of the pain, nor of the uneven roads. It was as if he were sleeping. And he was still in that drowsy state when he arrived at the emergency room of our hospital. . . . He woke up different, Esfandyar, without an arm and a leg, and he will remain different, a young disabled person in a country so poor that it cannot afford to care for him.

Since the early 1990s, when the movement to ban land mines became widespread, forty mine-producing countries stopped manufacturing them, and millions of land mines have been destroyed, the result being that the casualty rates dropped from 26,000 people a year to between 15,000 and 20,000. But fifteen countries still insist on producing land mines.

The United States maintains a stockpile of more than 10 million land mines and insists on the right to produce more and to use them when it sees fit. Both Democratic and Republican administrations consider the land mines strewn on the border between North and South Korea to be sacrosanct.

The Clinton administration made small steps in the direction of banning land mines but insisted that it must continue using "dumb mines" (which do not self-destruct after a period of time) until the year 2006, safely beyond Clinton's presidency. Bush has moved the year of eliminating these "dumb" mines to 2010, several years beyond the end of his own administration. The United States will continue to develop mines, but they will be "smart"

LAND MINES

mines, or, as the administration terms them, "non-persis-
tent" mines.

It should be noted that "smart" mines, according to a
briefing paper delivered at an international conference in
Nairobi by the director of Human Rights Watch's arms
division, are far from safe. These mines often fail to self-
destruct and "are usually used in great numbers, and spread
over huge areas, impossible to map or mark; while active,
they are indiscriminate, just like dumb mines."

The Bush administration bluntly explained why it would
not sign the mine ban treaty. "The United States will not
join . . . because its terms would have required us to give up
a needed military capability," the Bush administration said
in a fact sheet it released announcing its new policy. "Land
mines still have a valid and essential role protecting United
States forces in military operations."

Though 145 nations have signed the land mine treaty, we
certainly cannot expect that this war-hungry and militarized
government, whose slogan seems to be "Leave No Deadly
Weapon Behind," will follow suit on its own accord. Nor
can we expect it to realize the recklessness of resuming production of land mines. Only a national citizens' campaign
with people on all sides of the political spectrum (for who can
defend the use of weapons whose inevitable result is the
mutilation of children?) can bring about a change in land
mine policy.

The experience of Italy may be instructive. In the 1980s,
Italy sold millions of land mines to Iraq and Iran, which
were then at war with each other. Gino Strada's group,
Emergency, played a key role in launching a national cam-
paign against the land mines. It culminated in 1997 when
Italian citizens sent more than one million postcards to the

president of Italy. Each postcard carried a photo of a child mutilated by a land mine. That year the Italian parliament enacted a law banning the production, use, import, and export of land mines.

But Gino Strada understands that the campaign to ban land mines was treating the symptom of a deadly disease. The disease is war itself. One day, working in a hospital in Djibouti, Strada finds two victims from opposite sides of the civil war, in the same hospital, on beds three feet apart. One of them, though paralyzed, shouts that he wants to leave, refusing to lie alongside his enemy. Dr. Strada sits between the two of them and says: "I know nothing about this war. It is not my country, nor my culture. But I think that you two have paid enough, one paralyzed, the other without a leg. There can't be war anymore between the two of you; it is not possible anymore, even physically. You have good reasons, both of you, to hate war. Don't you think that war is the real enemy?"

Gino Strada knew of World War II only through his father's recollections in Milan. "My father told me of a school with many children inside, in the neighborhood of Gorla. It was hit by a bomb dropped from an airplane. 194 of them died, children with their teachers." He discovered that in the Second World War more than half of those who died were civilians.

Strada rejects the idea of "humanitarian wars," as I do. As mentioned earlier, I can accept that there may be rare situations where a small act of force might be used to halt a genocidal situation—Darfur and Rwanda are examples. But war, defined as the massive and indiscriminate use of force (and technology dictates that any large-scale use of force cannot be focused on a particular evil-doer) cannot be accepted, once you understand its human consequences.

Campaigns to rid the earth of land mines, napalm, white phosphorus, and depleted uranium, are important in themselves, as the reduction of symptoms is important to anyone suffering from a deadly illness. But those campaigns must be accompanied by the understanding that the illness itself must be eliminated.

Albert Einstein, horrified by the First World War, said: "War cannot be humanized. It can only be abolished."

For those like Gino Strada, who have seen with their own eyes the results of modern warfare, the abolition of war is not to be dismissed as utopian. The abolition of slavery in the United States was seen that way, but a handful of abolitionists—black and white—would not give up, and they eventually created a national movement powerful enough to turn a utopian dream into reality.

We also can realize the dream of a world without war, but only by stubborn persistence, only by a refusal to surrender that dream.

20

THE SUPREME COURT

On September 29, 2005, John Roberts was sworn in as the Supreme Court's seventeenth Chief Justice of the of the United States. Republican support was unanimous, Democrat opposition weak.

I heard the news and felt a sinking feeling. Listening to pieces of Roberts' confirmation hearings induced despair: the joking with the candidate, the obvious signs that, whether Democrat or Republican, all were members of the same exclusive club. Roberts's proper "credentials," his "nice guy" demeanor, his insistence to the Judiciary Committee that he is not an "ideologue" (can you imagine anyone, even Robert Bork or Dick Cheney, admitting that he is an "ideologue"?) were clearly more important than his views on equality, justice, the rights of defendants, or the war powers of the president.

At one point in the hearings the *New York Times* reported that Roberts "summed up his philosophy." He had been asked, "Are you going to be on the side of the little guy?" (Would any candidate admit that he was on the side of "the big guy"? Presumably serious "hearings" bring out idiot questions.)

Roberts replied: "If the Constitution says that the little guy should win, the little guy's going to win in court before me. But if the Constitution says that the big guy should win,

163

well, then the big guy's going to win, because my obligation is to the Constitution."

If the Constitution is the holy test, then a justice should abide by its provision in Article VI that not only the Constitution itself but "all Treaties made, or which shall be made, under the Authority of the United States, shall be the supreme Law of the Land." This includes the Geneva Conventions of 1949, which the United States signed and which insist that prisoners of war must be granted the rights of due process. A district court judge in 2004 ruled that the detainees held in Guantánamo for years without trial were protected by the Geneva Convention and deserved due process. Roberts and two colleagues on the Court of Appeals overruled this, but this decision was, in turn, overruled by a Supreme Court decision in June 2006, and a month later the Pentagon released new standards entitling military detainees to humane treatment and basic legal standards when they come to trial, as required by Common Article 3 of the Geneva Conventions.

There is enormous hypocrisy surrounding the pious veneration of the Constitution and "the rule of law." The Constitution, like the Bible, is infinitely flexible and is used to serve the political needs of the moment. When the country was in economic crisis and turmoil in the 1930s and capitalism needed to be saved from the anger of the poor, hungry, and unemployed, the Supreme Court was willing to stretch to infinity the constitutional right of Congress to regulate interstate commerce. It decided that the national government, desperate to regulate farm production, could tell a family farmer what to grow on his tiny piece of land.

When it gets in the way of a war, the Constitution is ignored. When the Supreme Court was faced, during

Vietnam, with a suit by soldiers refusing to go, claiming that there had been no declaration of war by Congress, as the Constitution requires, the soldiers could not even get four Supreme Court justices to agree to hear the case. When, during World War I, Congress ignored the First Amendment's right to free speech by passing legislation to prohibit criticism of the war, the imprisonment of dissenters under this law was upheld unanimously by the Supreme Court, which included two presumably liberal and learned justices: Oliver Wendell Holmes and Louis Brandeis.

It would be naïve to depend on the Supreme Court to defend the rights of poor people, women, people of color, and dissenters of all kinds. Those rights only come alive when citizens organize, protest, demonstrate, strike, boycott, rebel, and violate the law in order to uphold justice.

The distinction between law and justice is ignored by all those senators—Democrats and Republicans—who solemnly invoke as their highest concern "the rule of law." The law can be just; it can be unjust. It does not deserve to inherit the ultimate authority of the divine right of the king.

The Constitution gave no rights to working people: no right to work less than twelve hours a day, no right to a living wage, no right to safe working conditions. No right to treatment by a doctor when in need. No right to take time off to mourn a death or to celebrate a new birth. No right to a place to live. Workers had to organize, go on strike, and defy the law, the courts, and the police to create a great movement to win an eight-hour workday, and caused such commotion that Congress was forced to pass a minimum wage law, Social Security, and unemployment insurance.

The 1954 *Brown* decision on school desegregation did not come from a sudden realization of the Supreme Court that it was what the Fourteenth Amendment called for. After all, it was the same Fourteenth Amendment that had been cited in the 1896 *Plessy* case upholding racial segregation. It was the initiative of brave families in the South—along with the fear by the government, obsessed with the Cold War, that it was losing the hearts and minds of people of color all over the world—that brought a sudden enlightenment to the Court.

The Supreme Court in 1883 had interpreted the Fourteenth Amendment so that nongovernmental institutions such as hotels, restaurants, etc., could bar black people. But after the sit-ins and arrests of thousands of black people in the South in the early 1960s, the right to public accommodations was quietly given constitutional sanction by the Court in 1964. It now interpreted the interstate commerce clause, whose wording had not changed since 1787, to mean that places of public accommodation could be regulated by congressional action and be prohibited from discriminating. Soon this would include barbershops, and I suggest it takes an ingenious interpretation to include barbershops in interstate commerce.

Women's right to an abortion did not depend on the Supreme Court decision in *Roe v. Wade*. It was won before that decision, all over the country, by grassroots agitation that forced states to recognize the right. If the American people, who by a great majority favor that right, insist on it and act on it, no Supreme Court decision can take it away.

The rights of working people, women, and black people have not depended on decisions of the courts. Like the other branches of the political system, the courts have recognized these rights only after citizens have engaged in direct action powerful enough to win these rights for themselves.

This is not to say that we should ignore the courts or the electoral campaigns. It can be useful to get one person rather than another on the Supreme Court or in the White House or in Congress. The courts, win or lose, can be used to dramatize issues.

On St. Patrick's Day, 2003, on the eve of the invasion of Iraq, four antiwar activists poured their own blood around the vestibule of a military recruiting center near Ithaca, New York, and were arrested. Charged in state court with criminal mischief and trespassing (charges well suited to the American invaders of a certain Mideastern country), the St. Patrick's Four spoke their hearts to the jury. Peter DeMott, a Vietnam veteran, described the brutality of war. Danny Burns explained why invading Iraq would violate the UN Charter, a treaty signed by the United States. Clare Grady spoke of her moral obligations as a Christian. Teresa Grady spoke to the jury as a mother, telling them that women and children were the chief victims of war and that she cared about the children of Iraq. Nine of the twelve jurors voted to acquit them, and the judge declared a hung jury. When the federal government retried them on felony conspiracy charges, a jury acquitted them of those and convicted them on lesser charges.

Still, knowing the nature of the political and judicial system of this country, its inherent biases, we cannot become dependent on the courts or on our political leadership. Our culture—the media, the educational system—tries to crowd out of our political consciousness everything except who will be elected president and who will be on the Supreme Court, as if these are the most important decisions we make. They are not. They deflect us from the most important job citizens have, which is to energize democracy by organizing, protesting, sharing information, and engaging in acts of civil disobedience that shake up the system.

That is why the St. Patrick's Four need to be supported and emulated.

That is why the GIs refusing to return to Iraq, and the families of soldiers calling for withdrawal from the war, are so important.

That is why the demonstrations outside the White House and the peace marches in the streets of Washington bode well.

Let us not be disconsolate over the increasing control of the court system by the right wing. The courts have never been on the side of justice, only moving a few degrees one way or the other, unless pushed by the people. Those words engraved in the marble of the Supreme Court, "Equal Justice Before the Law," have always been a sham.

No Supreme Court, liberal or conservative, will stop the war in Iraq or redistribute the wealth of this country or establish free medical care for every human being. Such fundamental change, the experience of the past suggests, will depend on the actions of an aroused citizenry, demanding that the promise of the Declaration of Independence—an equal right to life, liberty, and the pursuit of happiness—be fulfilled.

21

CIVIL LIBERTIES DURING
WARTIME

Americans are proud of the Bill of Rights, and especially of the First Amendment to the Constitution, which declares that Congress may make no law "abridging the freedom of speech, or of the press. . . ." Not many Americans know that the First Amendment, while it looks good in print, becomes inoperable when our nation is at war or when there is some tense international situation short of war (a "Cold War").

It is ironic that exactly when a free marketplace of ideas is necessary, when matters of life and death are the issues, when Americans may be killed or may kill others, that our freedom of speech disappears. Yet that is exactly what the Supreme Court decided at the time of the First World War, when the venerable Oliver Wendell Holmes, speaking for a unanimous court, said that freedom of speech cannot be allowed if it creates "a clear and present danger" to the nation.

In fact, the case before the Supreme Court at that time was that of a man named Schenck, who had been imprisoned under the Espionage Act of 1917, which made it a crime to say or write things that would "discourage recruitment in the armed forces of the United States." The Espionage Act was interpreted by the courts to mean that any statement made in criticism of the United States' entry into World War I would constitute such discouragement and was therefore punishable by up to ten years in prison.

Long before the "clear and present danger" criterion was enunciated by Holmes, it was, in effect, operating to negate the First Amendment. Indeed, barely seven years after that amendment became part of the Constitution, Congress did exactly what the First Amendment said it could not do: "Congress shall make no law abridging the freedom of speech. . . ."

That was 1798, when, oddly enough, both the new revolutionary government in France and the new one in the United States were in a tense situation of "cold war." Congress passed the "Alien and Sedition Acts," which made it a crime to say anything "false, scandalous and malicious" about government officials "with intent to bring them into disrepute." A number of people who criticized President John Adams's administration were arrested and sent to prison under this act.

But it was in the twentieth century, and especially during World War I, that suppression of free speech made the constitutional guarantee meaningless. Two thousand people were prosecuted, and a thousand imprisoned, for speaking against the conscription law or against the war. An atmosphere was created in which it became very difficult to speak one's mind, either because of fear of government prosecution or because zealous citizens, catching the war fever, harassed and persecuted fellow citizens who opposed the war.

As an example of the absurdities that accompany wartime hysteria, the World War I period saw the prosecution of a filmmaker who made a movie about the American Revolution. Since the "enemy" in that movie was Britain, and since the United States was now allied with Britain, the court ruled that the film violated the Espionage Act. The title of the film was *The Spirit of '76*, and the name of the court case was *U.S. v. Spirit of '76*.

At the end of that war came the notorious Palmer raids, named after Attorney General A. Mitchell Palmer. Thousands of noncitizens were arrested, detained, and deported, without hearings or any of the due process guarantees of the Constitution.

World War II brought more repressive legislation in the form of the Smith Act, which made it a crime to "teach and advocate" the overthrow of the government by force and violence. During World War II, eighteen members of the Socialist Workers Party in Minneapolis were given prison terms, not for specifically advocating such ideas, but for distributing literature like the *Communist Manifesto*. And more than 100,000 Japanese Americans were put into detention camps, simply because of their national origin, a cruel act of wartime excitement.

The Cold War period that followed the Second World War created an atmosphere in which a hysterical fear of communism led to loyalty oaths for government employees, imprisonment for Communists, and jail terms for anyone refusing to answer questions put to them by the House Committee on Un-American Activities about their political affiliations. It was a time when the Federal Bureau of Investigation (FBI) was compiling lists of hundreds of thousands of Americans who had in some way registered their dissent from government policies. Congress passed legislation allowing for deportation of noncitizens who were members of organizations listed by the attorney general as subversive.

Although the United States was by far the most heavily armed nation in the world, there was an induced fear of the

Soviet Union, and then of Communist China, which enabled the government to ignore the Bill of Rights. The fear was far out of proportion to the actual danger, to the point where children were told to hide under their schoolroom desks as protection against nuclear bombs.

Thus, there is a long, dark history of loss of liberty in wartime that is a precedent for what has been happening in the United States since 9/11: the intimidating proliferation of American flags, illegal domestic spying, the harassment of Muslim people or anyone looking like a Middle Easterner, the mass detention of noncitizens, without trial or due process.

The question is, whether Americans will at some point begin to understand that the "war on terror" has also become a war against the liberties of Americans, and will demand that these liberties be restored. Without the right to speak freely, to dissent, we cannot evaluate what the government is doing, and so we may be swept into foreign policy adventures with no oppositional voices and later lament our silence.

22

SOLDIERS IN REVOLT

As the situation in Iraq worsens with increasing attacks on U.S. troops, increasing numbers of roadside bombs, and increasing casualties, there are growing signs of resistance from the ranks of U.S. servicemen and women who do not want to fight the war.

The United States has a long history of resistance from within the military. Probably the most astonishing examples came from Vietnam with the appearance of what came to called "fragging," the use of grenades and other explosive devices by disgruntled soldiers against their commanders. By the time U.S. soldiers were withdrawn from Vietnam in March 1973, there had been 86 deaths due to fragging.

In Vietnam, black soldiers and sailors were more prone to rebellion than others, and GIs who came from the working class were less enthusiastic about the war than those from more privileged backgrounds. In short, racial resentment and class anger fueled much of the disaffection from the war in Vietnam.

Historically, rebellion in the ranks long precedes Vietnam—from the Revolutionary War, the War with Mexico, the Civil War, the War with the Philippines and onward—although the antiwar activities of the Vietnam era were certainly the most massive, and the most successful in the nation's history.

In his book *Soldiers in Revolt,* David Cortright documents the rebellion of U.S. soldiers during the Vietnam years in stunning detail. Cortright's work is especially important to recall today because the war makers in the White House have been so anxious to put to rest what they call "the Vietnam syndrome." The word "syndrome" refers to a disease, in this case, the disease of popular opposition to a war of aggression fought against a small country half the world away.

The "disease" has shown up again, as more and more Americans declare their opposition to the war in Iraq. Surely, one of the factors in this national disapproval is the resemblance of the Iraq War to the war in Vietnam. The bombing and invasion of Iraq, the public has begun to realize, is not to defend the United States, but to control an oil-rich country already crushed by two wars and more than ten years of economic sanctions.

It is undoubtedly the nature of this war, so steeped in deceptions perpetrated on the American public—the false claims that Iraq possessed "weapons of mass destruction" and was connected to 9/11—that has provoked opposition to the war among the military. Further, the revelations of torture, the killing of Iraqi civilians, and the devastation of the country from bombardment, foreign occupation, and sectarian violence, to which many of the dissenting soldiers have been witness, contribute to their alienation.

A CBS News dispatch on December 6, 2004, reported on American GIs who have deserted the military and fled north across the border to live in Canada. Theirs were among the first 5,000 desertions that had occurred over the opening years of the war in Iraq. One soldier told the CBS journalist: "I didn't want 'Died deluded in Iraq' over my gravestone."

Jeremy Hinzman, of Rapid City, South Dakota, went to Canada after being denied conscientious objector status by the army. He told CBS: "I was told in basic training that, if I'm given an illegal or immoral order, it is my duty to disobey it, and I feel that invading and occupying Iraq is an illegal and immoral thing to do." His contract with the government, Hinzman said, was "to defend the Constitution of the United States, not take part in offensive, preemptive wars."

According to the *Toronto Globe & Mail* report on December 8, 2004: "Jimmy Massey, a former marine staff sergeant, told an immigration and refugee board hearing in Toronto that he and his fellow marines shot and killed more than thirty unarmed men, women and children, and even shot a young Iraqi who got out of his car with his arms in the air."

A *New York Times* story of March 18, 2005, told of an increasing number of soldiers seeking to escape duty in Iraq. One soldier, from Hinesville, Georgia, was reported to have asked a relative to shoot him in the leg so he would not have to return to war. The deserters in Canada, according to this story, came from various parts of the country but reported the same kind of motivations for wanting out of the military. "Some described grisly scenes from their first deployments to Iraq. One soldier said that he saw a wounded, weeping Iraqi child whom no one would help. . . . Others said they had simply realized that they did not believe in war, or at least not in this war."

Not all the dissension in the military has been due to an analysis of the moral nature of the war. As in other wars, very often, the soldiers simply feel maltreated by their officers, sent into dangerous situations without proper defenses, their lives considered cheap by higher-ups. On October 18, 2004, the *New York Times* reported that a platoon of eighteen men and women refused to deliver a shipment of fuel from one air base to another because they said their trucks were unsafe and lacked a proper armed escort.

In November 2004, the *New York Times* reported that the army was having trouble calling into duty members of the Individual Ready Reserve. These were former soldiers being ordered back into the military. And of 4,000 given notice to return to active duty, more than 1,800 of them requested exemptions. Furthermore, reports were multiplying, in the spring of 2005, of the difficulties army recruiters were finding in getting young people to enlist.

In early 2005, Naval Petty Officer Third Class Pablo Paredes refused to obey orders to board an assault ship in San Diego that was bound for the Persian Gulf. He told a U.S. Navy judge: "I believe as a member of the armed forces, beyond having a duty to my chain of command and my President, I have a higher duty to my conscience and to the supreme law of the land. Both of these higher duties dictate that I must not participate in any way, hands-on or indirect, in the current aggression that has been unleashed on Iraq."

For this, Paredes faced a year in the brig, but the navy judge, citing testimony about the illegality of the Iraq War, declined to give him jail time, instead gave him three months of hard labor, and reduced him in rank.

Especially disturbing are the stories of female soldiers who desert in order to escape sexual harassment by their male superiors. On June 26, 2006, National Public Radio reported the story of 21-year-old army specialist Suzanne Swift, who "deserted because of the sexual harassment she suffered during a year-long deployment to Iraq." Police arrested Swift at her home in Oregon and transferred her to

Fort Lewis, Washington. Since her story has been publicized in national media, Suzanne Swift's family has been contacted by scores of other female soldiers who have also been sexually harassed by fellow soldiers, but had not reported it.

In a reminder of the creation of the Vietnam Veterans Against the War, a number of men and women returning from Iraq formed Iraq Veterans Against the War. One of its founders, Kelly Dougherty, asked an audience at Harvard University in February of 2005 to follow the precedent of Vietnam protests. In Iraq, she felt: "I'm not defending freedom, I'm protecting a corporate interest."

The level of GI protest in the current Iraq War is still far from what it came to be during the war in Vietnam, but as the war in Iraq continues, a point may be reached where men and women in uniform can no longer tolerate the injustices they witness and experience. It is encouraging to be reminded of the basic desire of human beings to live at peace with one another other, once they have seen through the official lies and have developed the courage to resist the call to war.

23

THE COMING END OF THE
IRAQ WAR

The reality of active U.S. soldiers rebelling against the Iraq War is one of the strongest statements that the U.S. presence there is a disaster for the American people and an even bigger disaster for the Iraqi people.

It is a strange logic to declare, as so many in Washington do, that it was wrong for us to invade Iraq but right for us to remain. A *New York Times* editorial, a year into the war, summed up the situation accurately: "United States military forces remain essentially alone in battling what seems to be a growing insurgency, with no clear prospect of decisive success any time in the foreseeable future."

And then, in an extraordinary non sequitur: "Given the lack of other countries willing to put up their hands as volunteers, the only answer seems to be more American troops, and not just through the spring, as currently planned. . . . Forces need to be expanded through stepped-up recruitment."

Here is the flawed logic: the United States is utterly alone in this occupation. The insurgency continues to intensify. It is becoming more inconceivable each day that the United States, despite all its weaponry, will ever manage to overpower the resistance and quell the escalating violence in Iraq. There is no visible prospect of success. The definition of fanaticism is that when you discover that you are going in the wrong direction, you call it a "noble cause" and double your speed. President Bush calls it "staying the course."

Tens of thousands, more likely hundreds of thousands, have lost their lives so far, and we must not differentiate between "their" casualties and "ours" if we believe that all human beings have an equal right to life.

In 1967, the same arguments that we are hearing now were being made against withdrawal in Vietnam. The United States did not pull out its troops for six more years. During that time, the war killed at least one million more Vietnamese and perhaps 30,000 U.S. military personnel.

United States officials say again and again that we must stay in Iraq to bring stability and democracy to that country. Isn't it clear that after years of war and occupation we have brought only chaos and violence and death to that country, not any recognizable democracy?

Can democracy be nurtured by destroying cities, by bombing, by driving people from their homes?

There is no certainty as to what would happen in our absence. But there is absolute certainty about the result of our presence—escalating deaths on all sides.

The loss of life among Iraqi civilians is especially startling. In November 2004, the British medical journal *The Lancet* reported that up to 100,000 civilians had died so far as a result of the war, many of them children. In July 2006, the United Nations released a report documenting the civilian death toll in Iraq has escalated to 100 civilians killed *per day*, with no end in sight.

The statistics are cold and inadequate. According to a September 2004 Knight Ridder report, Dr. Mumtz Jaber, a vascular surgeon, told of his sister and brother-in-law driving and not stopping fast enough at an American checkpoint in Baghdad. Their three-year-old son was shot and killed. At the morgue in Baghdad, the physician there said he saw a family of eight brought in, three women, three men, two children. They had been sleeping on their roof because it was too hot inside when a military helicopter shot and killed them all.

One would have to multiply such individual stories by the thousands to grasp the reality of a military operation that claims only to be fighting against "terrorists" and "insurgents."

And what of those Iraqis—numbering more than ten thousand—who, simply on "suspicion," have been seized from their homes or the streets and put into indefinite detention, with no hearings, no right to attorneys, no charges? Some are released months later, without any explanation. The treatment ranges from ordinary humiliation to the sexual abuse and torture that took place by U.S. forces in Abu-Ghraib prison.

A February 2004 report by the International Committee of the Red Cross (ICRC) said about these detainees: "In almost all instances . . . arresting authorities provided no information about who they were . . . nor did they explain the cause of arrest. . . . Certain military intelligence officers told the ICRC that in their estimate, between eighty percent and ninety percent of the persons deprived of their liberty in Iraq had been arrested by mistake."

And what about the lives of those Iraqis who escape death and mutilation, or imprisonment? How do they live day by day? Imagine living under occupation without clean water, electricity, sewage disposal, or adequate health care. What the U.S. government has called the "reconstruction" of Iraq has become a sorry joke, a story of profiteering and corruption. A Reuters dispatch of August 2004 reported that an official U.S. audit found that more than eight billion dollars given to Iraqi ministries by the former U.S.-led authority could not be accounted for. How much more has been squandered in the years since then?

In the book *Twilight of Empire*, we find a collection of firsthand accounts, incisive essays, and poetry that presents the war in Iraq with a vivid intensity rarely matched in the literature on the war. Among the book's essays is one by Naomi Klein, who gives a clue to the reasons for this disaster. She describes how the U.S. government, with its utter devotion to the capitalist ethic of greed, has in effect turned the Iraqi economy over to multinational corporations, who have swarmed all over the country with only one thought in mind: profit. When the profit motive is primary, human needs are left behind.

Naomi Klein finds in Iraq a microcosm of what has been happening all over the world, where the power of the United States, the World Bank, and the International Monetary Fund have been used to turn public enterprises over to private corporations, insisting on deregulation, with calamitous results for ordinary people. While the press showed photos of poor people looting stores, she gives us the larger picture, the "economic looting" of Iraq by the multinationals.

No wonder that under the new statue that has replaced the dismantled statue of Saddam Hussein in Baghdad, someone has painted the words, in English: "All done. Go home."

Have we learned nothing from the history of imperial occupations, all pretending to help the people being occupied?

The United States, the latest of the great empires, is perhaps the most self-deluded, having forgotten that history of occupations, including our own: our fifty-year occupation of the Philippines, our long occupation of Haiti (1915–34) and of the Dominican Republic (1916–24), our military intervention in Southeast Asia, and our repeated interventions in Nicaragua, El Salvador, and Guatemala.

I have no doubt that the reason so many Americans still support the war is that they remain largely ignorant of U.S. history; they exhibit what Studs Terkel has called "our national amnesia." If there was some sense of history, the public would immediately connect the word "occupation" with World War II, since which time we have been familiar with the phrases "occupied France," "occupied Denmark," "occupied Europe." To recall that would be to suggest a shocking connection between Hitler's invasion of other countries (also claiming to "liberate" them) and the unprovoked U.S. invasion and occupation of Iraq. And then people might begin to understand why the Iraqis are violently resisting the American presence, recalling perhaps the "resistance movements" in France and elsewhere in Europe.

Many Americans also do not know the history of the Middle East, and Mike Davis reminds us, in another essay from *Twilight of Empire*, of the brutal British conquest of the very same lands now occupied by American and British forces. Does Tony Blair not feel a twinge of shame at the thought that he is engaging in a pitiful re-creation of those years after World War I, when English planes were bombing helpless villagers and Winston Churchill was proposing the use of poison gas against the resisting Arabs?

Davis reminds us that the "aerial terror" we have become accustomed to since Ethiopia and the Spanish Civil War and World War II—since Addis Ababa, Madrid, Dresden, Coventry, London, Tokyo, Hiroshima, Nagasaki—began in the Middle East with the bombing of Libya. And yes, the British Empire was "victorious," but at what horrific cost to the people of that region? And did not that victory ultimately end in ignominy?

Our military presence in Iraq is making us less safe, not more so. It is inflaming people in the Middle East, and thereby magnifying the danger of terrorism. Far from fighting "there rather than here," as President Bush has claimed, the occupation increases the chance that enraged infiltrators will strike us here at home.

As things get worse for ordinary Iraqis and for the U.S. occupation forces, President Bush continues to assure us that the war is winnable, and that it is being fought for a "noble cause."

The fact is, however, however, that Iraq is clearly not a liberated country, but an occupied country. American kids learn in school that it was the Nazis, then the Soviets, who occupied countries. The United States liberated them from occupation.

Now *we* are the occupiers. True, we liberated Iraq from Saddam Hussein, but not from us. Just as in 1898 we liberated Cuba from Spain, but not from us. Spanish tyranny was overthrown, but the U.S. established a military base in Cuba, as we are doing in Iraq. U.S. corporations moved into Cuba, just as Bechtel and Halliburton and the oil corporations have moved into Iraq. With support from local accomplices, the United States framed and imposed the constitution that would govern Cuba, just as it has drawn up, with help from local political groups, a constitution for Iraq. Not a liberation. An occupation.

And it's an ugly occupation. On August 7, 2003, the *New York Times* reported that General Sanchez in Baghdad was worried about the Iraqi reaction to occupation. Pro-U.S. Iraqi leaders were giving him a message, as he put it: "When you take a father in front of his family and put a bag over his head and put him on the ground, you have had a significant adverse effect on his dignity and respect in the eyes of his family." (That's very perceptive.)

We know that fighting during the U.S. offensive in November 2004 destroyed three-quarters of the town of Fallujah (population 360,000), killing hundreds of its inhabitants. The objective of the operation was to cleanse the town of the terrorist bands acting as part of a "Ba'athist conspiracy."

But we should recall that on June 16, 2003, barely six weeks after President Bush had claimed victory in Iraq, two reporters for the Knight Ridder newspaper group wrote this about the Fallujah area: "In dozens of interviews during the past five days, most residents across the area said there was no Ba'athist or Sunni conspiracy against U.S. soldiers, there were only people ready to fight because their relatives had been hurt or killed, or they themselves had been humiliated by home searches and road stops. . . ." One woman quoted in the article described how U.S. soldiers arrested her husband from their home because of empty wooden crates that they had bought for firewood. She exclaimed that it is the United States who is guilty of terrorism.

Soldiers who were set down in a country where they were told they would be welcomed as liberators and found that they were surrounded by a hostile population became fearful and trigger-happy. On March 4, 2005, nervous, frightened GIs guarding a roadblock fired at Italian journalist Giuliana Sgrena, who had just been released by kidnappers, and an Italian intelligence officer, Nicola Calipari, whom they killed.

There have been many reports of U.S. soldiers angry at being subject to the U.S. policy of "Stop Loss" and being forced to stay longer in the war. Such sentiments are becoming known to the U.S. public, as are the feelings of many deserters who are refusing to return to Iraq after home leave. A May 2003 Gallup poll reported that only 13 percent of the U.S. public thought the war was going badly. Three years later, in the summer of 2006, the level of public disapproval had mushroomed to 56 percent.

Unable to capture the perpetrators of the September 11 attacks, the United States invaded Afghanistan, killing thousands of people and driving hundreds of thousands from their homes. The United States still does not know where the main criminals are. Not knowing what weapons Saddam Hussein possessed, the United States invaded and bombed Iraq in March 2003, disregarding the UN, killing thousands of civilians and soldiers, and terrorizing the population; not knowing who was and was not a terrorist, the U.S. government has imprisoned hundreds of men and boys at Guantánamo Bay under such cruel conditions that three have successfully committed suicide (many try but are caught), and hundreds have gone on hunger strike.

The Amnesty International *Report 2005* notes: "Guantánamo Bay has become the gulag of our times. . . . When the most powerful country in the world thumbs its nose at the rule of law and human rights, it grants a license to others to commit abuse with impunity."

The Iraq War will undoubtedly claim many more victims, not only abroad but also on U.S. territory. The Bush administration maintains that, unlike the Vietnam War, this conflict is not causing many casualties. But when the war finally ends, the number of its indirect victims, through disease or mental disorders, will increase steadily. After the Vietnam War, veterans reported congenital malformations in their children caused by Agent Orange.

Officially there were only a few hundred losses in the First Gulf War of 1990–91, but the U.S. Gulf War Veterans Association has reported 8,000 deaths in the past ten years. Some 200,000 veterans, out of 600,000 who took part, have registered a range of complaints to the Veterans Administration, many of their illnesses owing to the weapons and munitions used in combat. We have yet to see the long-term effects of depleted uranium on those currently stationed in Iraq. In the current war, how many young men and women sent by Bush to liberate Iraq will come home with related illnesses?

Sooner or later, the war against Iraq, the assault on its people, and the occupation of its cities, will come to an end. In a sense, the process has already begun. Signs of mutiny have been appearing in Congress. Editorials calling for withdrawal from Iraq are increasingly common in the press. The antiwar movement has been growing, slowly but persistently, all over the country. The harsh realities have become visible. The troops will have to come home.

24

THE ENEMY IS WAR

The United States has not been invaded for almost 200 years, not since the year 1812, but it has invaded other countries, again and again, as it is doing at the present, and for that I feel shame. The world has been at war, again and again all through the twentieth century, and here it is, a new century, and we still have not done away with the horror of war. For that we should all feel ashamed. But that shame should not immobilize us. It should provoke us to action.

As Gino Strada writes in the final pages of his book *Green Parrots*, our mission must go beyond helping the victims of war, to abolishing war itself. He asks the question: "Is it monstrous to think about how to create the possibility of human relationships based on equality, on social justice, and on solidarity, and relationships from which the use of violence, terrorism and war is excluded by common accord?"

So let us think together about that possibility.

We must recognize that we cannot depend on the governments of the world to abolish war, because they and the economic interests they represent benefit from war. Therefore, we, the people of the world, must take up the challenge. And although we do not command armies, we do not have great treasuries of wealth, there is one crucial fact that gives us enormous power: the governments of the world cannot wage war without the participation of the people. Albert

Einstein understood this simple fact. Horrified by the carnage of the First World War in which 10 million died in the battlefields of Europe, Einstein said: "Wars will stop when men refuse to fight."

That is our challenge, to bring the world to the point where men and women will refuse to fight, and governments will be helpless to wage war.

Is that utopian? Impossible? Only a dream?

Do people go to war because it is part of human nature? If so, then we might consider it impossible to do away with war. But there is no evidence, in biology, or psychology, or anthropology, of a natural instinct for war. If that were so, we would find a spontaneous rush to war by masses of people. What we find is something very different: we find that governments must make enormous efforts to mobilize populations for war. They must entice young people with promises of money, land, education, skills. Immigrants are lured with promises of green cards and citizenship. And if those enticements don't work, government must coerce. It must conscript young people, force them into military service, threaten them with prison if they do not comply.

Woodrow Wilson found a citizenry so reluctant to enter the First World War that he had to pummel the nation with propaganda and imprison dissenters in order to get the country to join the butchery going on in Europe.

The most powerful weapon of governments in raising armies is the weapon of propaganda, of ideology. It must persuade young people, and their families, that though they may die, though they may lose arms or legs, or become blind, that it is done for the common good, for a noble cause, for democracy, for liberty, for God, for the country.

The idea that we owe something to our country goes far

back, to Plato, who puts into the mouth of Socrates the idea that the citizen has an obligation to the state, that the state is to be revered more than your father and mother. He says: "In war, and in the court of justice, and everywhere, you must do whatever your state and your country tell you to do, or you must persuade them that their commands are unjust." There is no equality here: the citizen may use persuasion, no more. The state may use force.

This idea of obedience to the state is the essence of totalitarianism. And we find it not only in Mussolini's Italy, in Hitler's Germany, in Stalin's Soviet Union, but in so-called democratic countries, like the United States.

I, too, was lured to enlist. During World War II, I became part of a crew on a B-17, a heavy bomber that flew out of England over the Continent. I dropped bombs on Berlin, on other cities in Germany, Hungary, Czechoslovakia, and even on a small town on the Atlantic coast of France. I never questioned anything I did. I believed fascism had to be resisted and defeated. I flew the last bombing missions of the war, received my Air Medal and my battle stars, and was quietly proud of my participation in the great war to defeat fascism. I had no doubts. I believed it was a just war.

And yet, when I packed up my things at the end of the war and put my old navigation logs and snapshots and other mementos into a folder, I marked that folder, almost without thinking, "Never Again."

I'm still not sure why I did that, but I suppose I was beginning, unconsciously, to do what I would later do consciously: question the motives, conduct, and consequences of that crusade against fascism. It was not that my abhorrence of fascism was in any way diminished. But that clear certainty of moral rightness that propelled me into the air force as an enthusiastic bombardier was now clouded over by many thoughts.

Perhaps the doubts started in the midst of my bombing missions during my conversations with a gunner on another crew, a reader of history with whom I had become friends. To my astonishment, he would say to me, "You know this is an imperialist war. The fascists are evil. But our side is not much better." I could not accept his statement at the time, but it stuck with me. He believed that Britain and the United States were opposing fascism only because it threatened their own control over resources and people.

I began to think about the motives of the Western powers and Stalinist Russia and wondered if they cared as much about fascism as about retaining their own empires, their own power, and if that was why they had military priorities higher than bombing the rail lines leading to Auschwitz. Six million Jews were killed in the death camps (allowed to be killed?). Only 60,000 were saved by the war: 1 percent.

Yes, Hitler was a maniacal dictator and invader of other countries. But what of the British and their long history of wars against native peoples to subdue them for the profit and glory of the Empire? And the Soviet Union—was it not also a brutal dictatorship, concerned not with the working classes of the world but with its own national power? And what of my own country, with its imperial ambitions in Latin America and Asia? The United States had entered the war not when the Japanese were committing atrocities against China, but only when Japan attacked Pearl Harbor in Hawaii, a colony of the United States.

These were troubling questions, but I continued to fly my bombing missions. Ironically, my radical friend who called it an imperialist war was killed in a mission over Germany not long after our conversation.

When the war in Europe ended, my crew flew back to the United States in the same plane we used for our bombing missions. We were given a 30-day leave and then were supposed to go to the Pacific to fly bombing missions against the Japanese. My wife and I had been married before I went overseas. We decided to spend some time in the countryside before I had to go to the Pacific. On the way to the bus station we passed a news stand. It was August 7, 1945. There was a huge headline: ATOMIC BOMB DROPPED ON HIROSHIMA, CITY DESTROYED. I had no idea what an atomic bomb was, but I remember my feeling at the time, a sense of relief; the war would be over soon, I would not have to go to the Pacific.

Shortly after the war ended, something important happened to cause me to think differently about Hiroshima and also to rethink my belief that we had been engaged in a "just war." I read the report of a journalist, John Hersey, who went into Hiroshima shortly after the bombing and talked to survivors. You can imagine what those survivors looked like—some without arms, others without legs, others blinded, or with their skin so burned that you could not look at them. I read their stories, and for the first time I realized the human consequences of bombing.

When I was discharged from the air force, I received a letter from General George Marshall, commander of all the armed forces, congratulating me and the 16 million other Americans who had served in the military, and telling me it would now be a different world. But as the years went it became more and more clear that it was not a different world. I came to the conclusion that war, even a victorious war over an evil enemy—as in the war against fascism—is a quick fix, like a drug, which gives you a rush of euphoria, but when it wears away you are back in the depths and you must have another fix, another war. In his second term as president, George Bush admitted that the United States is "addicted to oil." What he did not also confess is that our government is also addicted to war.

If we want to break that addiction we need to teach history, because when you look at the history of wars, you see how war corrupts everyone involved, how the so-called good side behaves like the bad side, and how this has been true from the Peloponnesian War all the way to our own time.

While we Americans continue to pressure the government to end the war in Iraq, should we not think beyond this war? Should we not begin speaking about ending not just this war or that war, but war itself?

There is something important to be learned from the recent experience of the United States and Israel in the Middle East: massive military attacks, inevitably indiscriminate, are not only morally reprehensible but useless in achieving the stated aims of those who carry them out. The United States, in more than three years of war, which began with shock-and-awe bombardment and goes on with day-to-day violence and chaos, has been an utter failure in its claimed objective of bringing democracy and stability to Iraq. The Israeli invasion and bombing of Lebanon has not brought security to Israel; indeed, it has increased the number of its enemies, whether in Hezbollah or Hamas or among Arabs who belong to neither of those groups. These views are, in fact, supported by the most recent U.S. National Intelligence Estimate, conclusions from which were leaked to the media in September 2006, and which assert that the U.S. invasion and occupation of Iraq has not decreased, but increased the spread and threat of terrorism and radical jihad ideology.

I remember John Hersey's novel, *The War Lover*, in which a macho American pilot, who loves to drop bombs on people and also to boast about his sexual conquests, turns out to be impotent. President Bush, strutting in his flight jacket on an aircraft carrier and announcing victory in Iraq, has turned out to be much like the Hersey character, his words equally boastful, his military machine impotent. The history of wars fought since the end of World War II reveals the futility of large-scale violence.

Even the "victories" of great military powers turn out to be elusive. Presumably, after attacking and invading Afghanistan, the president was able to declare that the Taliban were defeated. But more than four years later, Afghanistan is rife with violence, and the Taliban are active in much of the country.

Beyond the futility of armed force, and ultimately more important, is the fact that war in our time inevitably results in the indiscriminate killing of large numbers of people. To put it more bluntly, war is terrorism. That is why a "war on terrorism" is a contradiction in terms. Wars waged by nations, whether by the United States or Israel, are a hundred times more deadly for innocent people than the attacks by terrorists, vicious as they are. The repeated excuse, given by both Pentagon spokespersons and Israeli officials, for dropping bombs where ordinary people live is that terrorists hide among civilians. Therefore the killing of innocent people (in Iraq, in Lebanon) is called accidental, whereas the deaths caused by terrorists (on 9/11, by Hezbollah rockets) are deliberate.

This is a false distinction, quickly refuted with a bit of thought. If a bomb is deliberately dropped on a house or a vehicle on the grounds that a "suspected terrorist" is inside (note the frequent use of the word "suspected" as evidence of the uncertainty surrounding targets), the resulting deaths of women and children may not be intentional. But neither are they accidental. The proper description is "inevitable."

So if an action will inevitably kill innocent people, it is as immoral as a deliberate attack on civilians. And when you consider that the number of innocent people dying inevitably in "accidental" events has been far, far greater than all the deaths deliberately caused by terrorists, one must reject war as a solution for terrorism.

Again, I acknowledge the possibility of humanitarian intervention to prevent atrocities, as in Sudan. But war, defined as the indiscriminate killing of large numbers of people, must be resisted.

I don't believe that our government will be able to do once more what it did after Vietnam: prepare the population for still another plunge into violence and dishonor. It seems to me that when the war in Iraq ends, and the war syndrome heals, that there will be a great opportunity to make that healing permanent.

My hope is that the memory of death and disgrace will be so intense that the people of the United States will be able to listen to a message that the rest of the world, sobered by wars without end, can also understand: that war itself is the enemy of the human race.

Governments will resist this message. But their power is dependent on the obedience of the citizenry. When we withdraw our obedience, the government will be helpless. We have seen this again and again in history.

The abolition of war has become not only desirable but necessary if the planet is to be saved. It is an idea whose time has come.

25

GOVERNMENTS LIE

When the great journalist I. F. Stone was asked by journalism students for advice, he had two words: "Governments lie."

Now that most Americans no longer believe in the war nor trust Bush and his administration, and evidence of official deception has become old news, we might ask: why were so many people so easily fooled?

The question is important because it might help us understand why Americans—members of the media as well as the ordinary citizen—rushed to declare their support as the president was sending troops halfway around the world to Iraq.

A small example of the innocence (or obsequiousness, to be more exact) of the press is the way it reacted to Secretary of State Colin Powell's presentation in February 2003 to the UN Security Council, a month before the invasion, a speech that may have set a record for the number of falsehoods told in one talk. In it, Powell confidently rattled off his "evidence": satellite photographs, audio records, reports from informants, with precise statistics on how many gallons of this and that existed for chemical warfare. The *New York Times* was breathless with admiration. The *Washington Post* editorial was titled "Irrefutable" and declared that after Powell's talk "it is hard to imagine how anyone could doubt that Iraq possesses weapons of mass destruction."

The truth was that a small army of UN inspectors could not find weapons of mass destruction in Iraq. A large army of 100,000 soldiers marauding through the country could not find them. But back in February 2003 the White House said: "We know for a fact that there are weapons there." Vice President Dick Cheney said on *Meet the Press*: "[W]e believe Saddam has in fact, reconstituted nuclear weapons." On March 30, 2003, Rumsfeld said on ABC TV: "We know where they are." And Bush said on Polish TV: "We've found the weapons of mass destruction."

The only weapons of mass destruction in Iraq turned out to be ours: bombs and missiles raining down by the thousands, cluster bombs spewing out deadly pellets, the arsenal of the greatest military power on earth visiting destruction on yet another country.

Self-determination for the Iraqis becomes an ironic claim as the new officialdom, headed by wealthy exiles, is flown by U.S. planes into Iraq and positions of power. In Vietnam there was a similar claim as Ngo Dinh Diem was flown into Saigon to rule South Vietnam in the interest of U.S. hegemony in Southeast Asia.

It seems to me there are two reasons, which go deep into our national culture, and which help explain the vulnerability of the press and of the citizenry to outrageous lies whose consequences bring death to tens of thousands of people. If we can understand those reasons, we can better guard ourselves against being deceived in the future.

One reason is in the dimension of time, that is, an absence of historical perspective. The other is in the dimension of space, that is, an inability to think outside the boundaries of nationalism. We are penned in by the arrogant perspective that this country is the center of the universe, exceptionally virtuous, admirable, superior.

If we don't know history, then we are ready meat for carnivorous politicians, intellectuals, and journalists who supply the carving knives. I am not speaking of the history we learned in the public school system, a history subservient to our political leaders, from the much-admired Founding Fathers to the presidents of recent years. I mean a history that is honest about the past. If we don't know that history, then any president can stand up to the battery of microphones and declare that we must go to war, and we will have no basis for challenging him. He—or she—will say that the nation is in danger, that democracy and liberty are at stake, and that we must therefore send ships and planes to destroy our new enemy, and we will have no reason to disbelieve that president.

But if we know some history, if we know how many times presidents have made similar declarations to the country, and how they turned out to be lies, we will not be fooled. Although some of us may pride ourselves that we were never fooled, we still might accept as our civic duty the responsibility to buttress our fellow citizens against the mendacity of our high officials.

We would remind whoever we can that President Polk lied to the nation about the reason for going to war with Mexico in 1846. It wasn't that Mexico "shed American blood upon the American soil," but that Polk, and the slave-owning aristocracy, coveted half of Mexico.

We would point out that President McKinley lied in 1898 about the reason for invading Cuba, saying we wanted to liberate the Cubans from Spanish control, but the truth is that the United States really wanted Spain out of Cuba so that the island could be open to United Fruit and other American corporations. He also lied about the reasons for our war in the Philippines, claiming we only wanted to "civilize" the Filipinos, while the real reason was to own a valuable piece of real estate in the far Pacific, even if we had to kill hundreds of thousands of Filipinos in order to accomplish that.

President Woodrow Wilson lied about the reasons for entering the First World War, saying it was a war to "make the world safe for democracy," when it was really a war to make the world safe for the Western imperial powers.

Harry Truman lied to the nation and the world when he described Hiroshima—which he had just devastated with an atomic blast—as "an important Japanese Army base." More than 100,000 civilians—men, women, and children—died in what was then a city of 350,000.

Truman also lied to the nation about our war in Korea, saying we were fighting for democracy (hardly, since South Korea was a military dictatorship). More than 50,000 Americans and perhaps 2 million Koreans died as a result.

Dwight D. Eisenhower lied about our spy flights over the Soviet Union, even after one flier on such a mission was shot down. He deceived the nation and the world about the U.S. involvement in the coup that overthrew a democratic government in Guatemala. That coup brought on a succession of military juntas that took tens of thousands of lives. Eisenhower deceived the nation about the U.S. role in subverting a government in Iran because it was offending multinational oil corporations. The United States put the shah of Iran back on the throne, and his secret police tortured and executed thousands of his opponents.

John F. Kennedy lied to the nation about U.S. involvement in the 1961 failed invasion of Cuba, telling a press conference: "I can assure you that the United States has no intention of using force to overthrow the Castro regime."

Everyone lied about Vietnam. Kennedy said the United States was not involved in the overthrow of Ngo Dinh Diem. Kennedy also repeatedly claimed that American fliers were not involved in the bombing of Vietnam, even though he sent two helicopter companies there as early as 1962, with the U.S. military dropping napalm shortly thereafter.

Johnson and Nixon both lied when they claimed only military targets were bombed (reporters knew the greatest number of deaths was among civilians). And Nixon deceived the nation about the secret bombing of Cambodia.

Reagan lied to the nation about his covert and illegal support of the contras in Nicaragua. He lied about the importance of Grenada in order to justify the 1983 invasion of that little island.

George Bush lied about the reasons for invading Panama in 1989, saying it was to stop the drug trade. In fact, the United States has allowed the drug trade to flourish. Bush also deceived the nation about his real interest in the Persian Gulf. He pretended to be anguished about the fate of Kuwait while he was actually more concerned about enhancing American power in Saudi Arabia and controlling the region's oil deposits.

Given the overwhelming record of lies told to justify wars, how could anyone listening to the younger Bush believe him as he laid out the reasons for invading Iraq?

And what of Clinton's deceptions? Against the history of lies that have brought death to so many people, Clinton's deceptions about sex in the Oval Office were ludicrous. But those were all that his Republican enemies and pundits cared about.

Clinton had his own share of lies and deceits about lethal public policy. But he never got into trouble for those.

People who are indignant that he lied about his affair with Monica Lewinsky were silent when he deceived the nation about the need to bomb a "nerve gas plant" in Sudan. His administration could produce no evidence that the plant was anything but what the Sudanese government said it was—a plant that produced medicines for the Sudanese people.

Where was the criticism of Clinton when he signed a crime bill to build more prisons and execute more people on the falsehood that these acts will deter crime?

Where was the criticism of Clinton when he approved the attack on the Waco compound, which led to the deaths of eighty-one people, arguing erroneously that it was the only alternative?

Where was the criticism of Clinton when his administration refused to join the international ban on land mines or authorize a strong world court on the specious grounds that the United States would be in jeopardy?

Where was the criticism of Clinton when he defended Boris Yeltsin's brutal attack on Chechnya by obscenely comparing it to Abraham Lincoln's war to unify the states?

A careful reading of history might give us another safeguard against being deceived. It would make clear that there has always been, and is today, a profound conflict of interest between the government and the people of the United States. When the eminent historian Charles Beard suggested, a hundred years ago, that the Constitution represented not the working people, not the slaves, but the slaveholders, the merchants, the bondholders, he became the object of an indignant editorial in the *New York Times*.

The facts are embarrassing but must be faced if we are to be honest. We must face our long grim history of ethnic cleansing, slavery, racism, imperial conquest, and acts of unwarranted intervention and aggression around the world.

Our leaders, on the other hand, continue to plant the belief that we are entitled, because of our moral superiority, to dominate the world.

What is the idea of our moral superiority based on? Surely not on our behavior toward people in other parts of the world. Is it based on how well people in the United States live? One of five children in this, the richest country in the world, is born in poverty. There are more than forty countries that have better records on infant mortality. Cuba does better. And it is a sure sign of sickness in society when we lead the world in the number of people in prison—more than 2 million.

A more honest estimate of ourselves as a nation would prepare us all for the next barrage of lies that will accompany the next proposal to inflict our power on some other part of the world. It might also inspire us to create a different history for ourselves, by taking our country away from the liars and killers who govern it and by rejecting nationalist arrogance, so that we can join the rest of the human race in the common cause of peace and justice.

26

THE LONG WAR

Among our government's biggest ongoing lies must be that we are "winning the war on terror," recently rebranded "The Long War." "Our progress," President Bush said, two years into the war in Iraq, "is a tribute to the might of the United States military." My hometown newspaper, the *Boston Globe*, was congratulatory: "On the war front, the administration has much to take pride in."

But the president has also told us that "tens of thousands of trained terrorists are still at large." That hardly suggests we are "winning the war." Furthermore, he has said that there is a "grave and growing danger."

Bush has singled out Iran and North Korea as well because they are trying to develop "weapons of mass destruction." And that's not all; "Terror training camps still exist in at least a dozen countries," he has said.

The prospect is for a war without end. General Kimmitt, U.S. Central Command deputy director of plans and strategy, told BBC News in April 2006 that "[e]ven if Iraq stabilised tomorrow the Long War would continue." In no previous administration has a president ever talked about such a war. Indeed, presidents have been anxious to assure the nation that the sacrifices demanded would be finite, and as each war went on, we were told, as in Vietnam, there was "light at the end of the tunnel."

No light is visible in this "long war" on terrorism, for, as the president says, "These enemies view the entire world as a battlefield, and we must pursue them wherever they are."

It seems necessary for the nation to remain frightened. The enemy is everywhere. "The campaign may not be finished on our watch," Bush says. He will pass on the job to the next president, and perhaps the next and the next.

This is an elusive enemy, whose defeat requires an open-ended war. And so long as the nation is in a state of war, it is possible to demand of the American people certain sacrifices.

Immediately, we must sacrifice our freedoms (although the war is presumably to protect freedom). "We choose freedom and the dignity of every life," the president said. But we cannot choose freedom now. For now, we must give up the freedoms promised by our Bill of Rights.

The USA PATRIOT Act and related laws gave the government sweeping new powers to keep watch over us, enlarging its right to spy with wiretaps and computer surveillance, and allowing officials to conduct secret searches of homes and offices. When these new powers were not sufficient, the government spied on us in violation of the law, as has been reported widely in the press since late 2005.

The secretary of state can designate any organization as a terrorist organization, and his decision is not subject to review. The USA PATRIOT Act defines a "domestic terrorist" as someone who violates the law and is engaged in activities that "appear to be intended to . . . influence the policy of government by intimidation or coercion." This could make many activist organizations subject to designation as terrorist organizations. Immigrants who do not yet have green cards—and there are 20 million of them in the

United States—are subject to roundups, raids, indefinite detention, and deportation.

So we now have all sorts of enemies to fear: noncitizens and dissidents at home; an infinite number of mysterious enemies abroad. We will have to concentrate not only our resources but our attention on that endless war. We will be looking everywhere in the world for our enemies.

We will not be paying attention to the thousands who die in this country not at the hands of terrorists but because of the profit system, the "free market." When I spoke recently on a radio show in Madison, Wisconsin, a caller asked why, grieving as we all have for the thousands of victims of the September 11 action, do we not also grieve the thousands of people who die on the job in industrial accidents?

We could extend that question and ask why are we not grieving also for the thousands of children who die every year in this country for lack of food and medical care?

The answer seems clear. To do that would call attention not to obscure foreign terrorists but to a system of corporate domination in which executive profit comes before worker safety. It would call attention to a political system in which the government can fund hundreds of billions for its military machine but cannot find the money to give free health care, decent housing, minimum family incomes—all those requisites for children to grow up healthy.

It is right to mourn the deaths of 3,000 people who died at the hands of terrorists. But we should also know that every day, according to the UN World Food Programme, 11,000 children die of hunger around the world.

In a recent report entitled "Determinants of Malnutrition," the World Health Organization said: "All too frequently, the poor in fertile developing countries stand by watching with empty hands—and empty stomachs—while ample harvests and bumper crops are exported for hard cash. Short-term profits for a few, long-term losses for many. Hunger is a question of maldistribution and inequality, not lack of food."

The economist and Nobel Laureate Amartya Sen has written: "Global capitalism is much more concerned with expanding the domain of market relations than with, say, establishing democracy, expanding elementary education, or enhancing the social opportunities of society's underdogs."

The hundreds of millions of people in the United States and the rest of the world who are without medical care or food or work are the collateral damage of what Pope John Paul II once called "savage, unbridled capitalism." That damage is kept out of sight by the "war on terror." The war not only provides huge profits to military contractors and power to the politicians, but it also blocks out the conditions of people's lives, here and abroad.

What shall we do? We start with the core problem: there is immense wealth available, enough to care for the urgent needs of everyone on Earth, and this wealth is being monopolized by a small number of individuals, who squander it on luxuries and war while millions die and millions more live in misery and squalor.

This is a problem understood by people everywhere, because it has a simplicity absent in issues of war and nationalism. That is, people know with supreme clarity—when their attention is not concentrated on waging war by the government and the media—that the world is run by the rich and that money decides politics, culture, and some of the most intimate human relations.

The evidence for this is piling up and becoming harder to put aside.

The exposé and collapse of the gargantuan Enron Corporation—with its wholesale loss of jobs and the sudden disappearance of health insurance and retirement pensions—points to an economic system that is inherently corrupt.

The sudden impoverishment of Argentina, one of the richest countries in Latin America, provides more evidence. We are seeing the results of "the free market" and "free trade" and the demands for "privatization" in the rules of the World Bank and the International Monetary Fund. Instead of the public's taking charge of basic services—water, heat, transportation—private companies have taken over, and the results have been disastrous (as in Bolivia and other countries). In the case of Argentina, a French company took over the water system and quadrupled the fees charged for water.

While criticizing the war on terror and exposing its many hypocrisies, we need to realize that if we do only that, we, too, become victims of the war. We, too—like so many Americans listening to the president's frightening view of enemies here, there, everywhere—will have been diverted from an idea that could unite Americans as surely as fear of terrorists.

The idea is a startling one, but immediately recognizable as true: our most deadly enemies may not be hiding in caves and compounds abroad but in the corporate boardrooms and governmental offices where decisions are made that consign millions to death and misery—not deliberately, but as collateral damage of the lust for profit and power.

To overcome these enemies we will need the spirit of Seattle and Pôrto Alegre, a reinvigorated labor movement, a mobilization of people across the rainbow, the beginning of global solidarity, looking to a long-delayed sharing of the fruits of the Earth.

27

A BREAK-IN FOR PEACE

In the film *Ocean's 11*, eleven skillful crooks embark on an ingenious plan, meticulously worked out, to break into an impossibly secure vault and make off with more than 100 million dollars in Las Vegas casino loot. Hardly a crime of passion, despite the faint electrical charge surrounding Julia Roberts and George Clooney. No, money was the motive, with as little moral fervor attending the crime as went into the making of the movie, which had the same motive.

I was reminded of this recently when I sat in a courtroom in Camden, New Jersey, and participated in the recollection of another break-in, carried out by the Camden 28, where the motive was to protest the war in Vietnam.

It was the summer of 1971 when a group of men and women, ranging from young to middle-aged, including a few Catholic priests, carefully worked out a plan (going over building diagrams and armed with walkie-talkies, just like the *Ocean's 11*) to break into the draft board offices on the fifth floor of the federal building in Camden and make off with thousands of draft records. It was an act of symbolic sabotage, designed to dramatize the anguish felt over the death and suffering taking place in Vietnam.

It was a crime of passion, not the sort Hollywood is likely to make a movie about, but young documentary filmmaker named Anthony Giacchino decided to tell the story. It happens that his family in Camden attended the Church of the Sacred Heart, whose priest is Father Michael Doyle, one of the Camden 28.

One spring day in 2002 I received a phone call from Anthony, who asked if I could show up in Camden on May 4 for a retrospective of the event. I had been a witness in the 1973 trial. He told me most of the twenty-eight defendants would be there, as well as David Kairys and Martin Stolar, who had helped them in acting as their attorneys in the trial. The judge who presided in the 1971 trial, Clarkson Fisher, was dead. So was John Barry, who prosecuted the case. But a representative of the FBI would be present, along with one member of the jury.

We would all be meeting in the same courtroom where the trial took place, two floors below where the Camden 28 made their way into the draft board office and stuffed draft records into mail bags. This surprising arrangement was possible because the Historical Society of the Federal District Court for New Jersey had decided to do video histories of the important trials that had taken place in that courthouse. And the series would start with the most famous of those trials, that of the Camden 28.

On August 22, 1971, "eight figures in dark clothes scaled a ladder to the top of the U.S. Post Office Building in Camden, the home of the federal court and the local draft board," the *Philadelphia Inquirer* reported. "They carried burglar tools and a strong belief that the war in Vietnam was wrong."

It was about 2:30 a.m., and they had decided to do it then so there would be no encounter with people working there, no chance of violence. But they encountered 100 FBI agents, tipped off by Robert Hardy, who had been a friend of some of the defendants. Hardy was an informant and agent provocateur, supplying the group with the necessary equipment for the break-in. In the midst of the trial, Hardy's daughter was killed in an accident. He asked Father Doyle to perform the funeral service. It was, in some sense, a turning point in Hardy's role. Finally, he decided to testify for the defendants that he had acted for the FBI to entrap them into their action.

What was unusual about the trial was that the defendants were able to do what had not been possible in the previous trials of draft board raiders (the Baltimore 4, the Catonsville 9, the Milwaukee 14, and many others). In those trials, the judges had insisted that the war could not be an issue, that the jury must consider what was done as ordinary crimes: breaking and entering, arson (where draft records were burned, as in Catonsville), and destruction of government property.

In Camden, Judge Fisher did not forbid discussion of the war. The defendants were allowed to fully present the reasons for their action—that is, their passionate opposition to the war in Vietnam. And they made the most of this.

Father Doyle, at the time a newly arrived immigrant from Ireland, persuaded Judge Fisher to allow him to present film clips to the jury. Some showed Vietnam villages bombed, in flames; others showed sections of Camden looking like a bombed out city. He talked about Camden, a city of poverty and violence, where thirty-one of its young men were killed in Vietnam. "The sons of the rich never went there," he said.

Called as a witness, Daniel Berrigan read a poem he had written while in Vietnam, "Children in the Shelter," which ends with these lines:

I picked up the littlest
a boy, his face
breaded with rice (His sister calmly
*   feeding him*
as we climbed down)

In my arms, fathered
in a moment's grace, the messiah
of all my tears. I bore, reborn

a Hiroshima child from hell.

Another defense witness, surprisingly, was Major Clement St. Martin, who had been in charge of the state induction center in Newark, New Jersey, from 1968 to 1971. He described in detail how the draft system discriminated systematically against the poor, the black, and the uneducated, and how it regularly gave medical exemptions to the sons of the wealthy.

Major St. Martin said he thought all draft files should be destroyed. Asked, under cross-examination, if he thought private citizens had a right to break into buildings to destroy draft files, he replied: "Probably today, if they plan another raid, I might join them."

A Vietnamese woman named Tran Khanh Tuyet testified for the defendants, describing her life in South Vietnam, and told a hushed courtroom: "In the name of liberty you have destroyed my country."

One of the defendants, Cookie Ridolfi, at that time a working-class young woman from Philadelphia, now a law professor in California, put it bluntly: "We are not here because of a crime committed in Camden, but because of a war waged in Indochina."

It was Ridolfi who had phoned me one day in 1971 to ask if I would appear in the Camden trial as her witness. I had just returned from Los Angeles, where I had testified in the Pentagon Papers trial of Daniel Ellsberg and Anthony Russo.

In my previous appearances as a witness for defendants in draft board cases, judges had strictly forbidden testimony relating to the war or to civil disobedience. To my surprise, Judge Fisher allowed me to testify for several hours. I recounted what the Pentagon Papers told us about the history of the Vietnam War and discussed in detail the theory and history of civil disobedience in the United States. I said that the war was not being fought for freedom and democracy; the internal memoranda of the government spoke instead, again and again, of "tin, rubber, oil."

The day after my testimony in Camden, one of the defendants, Bob Good, called his mother, Mary Good, to the stand.

Mrs. Good was a conservative woman, a devout Catholic. She considered herself a patriot. One of her sons, Paul, had been killed in Vietnam.

On the witness stand, she told the jury, "I'm proud of my son because he didn't know. To take that lovely boy and to tell him, 'You are fighting for your country'—How stupid can you get? Can anybody stand here and tell me how he was fighting for his country? I can't understand what we're doing over there. We should get out of this. But not one of us, not a one of us, raised our hands to do anything about it. We left it up to these people, for them to do it. And now we are prosecuting them for it. God!"

Michael Giocondo, who had been a Franciscan priest in Costa Rica before he joined the Camden group, asked the jury: "What is more important, the pieces of paper that were the draft records, or the children of Vietnam?"

The jurors reacted in remarkable ways. Samuel Braithwaite, a fifty-three-year-old black taxi driver, a veteran of eleven years in the army, sent questions up to the bench (a right that jurors have but almost never exercise) to be put to the witnesses. One of his questions, which he said was directed to "all men of the clergy," was: "Didn't God make the Vietnamese? Was God prejudiced and only made American people?" Another of Braithwaite's questions: "If, when a citizen violates the law, he is punished by the government, who does the punishing when the government violates the law?

At the reunion in Camden, Peter Fordi, once a Jesuit priest, told how he and the other defendants stood in the courtroom, linking arms as the jury filed in, after two days of deliberation. His voice broke as he recalled the verdict, "Not Guilty" on all charges, and how then there was pandemonium in the courtroom, cheering and weeping and people hugging one another. And how then everyone stood, including the court marshals and the members of the jury, and sang "Amazing Grace." And how the word spread out of the courtroom into the street where a crowd had gathered and now cheered the verdict.

Mary Good also came back to Camden and reenacted her earlier appearance as her son's witness. When she finished, the entire courtroom, including the FBI man, stood and applauded.

The acquittal of the Camden 28 was a historic event. Supreme Court Justice William Brennan referred to it later as "one of the great trials of the twentieth century." It was the first time, in the many trials of antiwar activists who had broken into draft boards, that a jury had voted to acquit.

Why? No doubt because it was the first of these trials in which the jury had been permitted to listen to the heartfelt stories of fellow citizens as they described their growing anguish for the victims, American and Vietnamese, of a brutal war. And the jury was led to understand how the defendants could decide to break the law in order to dramatize their protest.

Most importantly, the year of the trial was 1973. By then the majority of the American people had turned against the war. They had seen the images of the burning villages and napalmed children and had begun to see through the deceptions of the nation's political leaders.

As today we are a nation at war, it is good to keep in mind that things can change. People learn, little by little. Lies are exposed. Wars once popular gradually come under suspicion. That happens when enough people speak and act in accord with their conscience, appealing to the American jury with the power of truth.

When the Camden trial was over, the black taxi driver on the jury, Samuel Braithwaite (now dead), left a letter for the defendants: "I say, well done. . . ."

28

PHIL BERRIGAN: HOLY OUTLAW

The long funeral procession for Phil Berrigan moved slowly through the streets of the poor black parish in Baltimore where he had begun his priesthood. Some parents held young children by the hand as they walked behind the flatbed truck that carried Phil's coffin, which had been made by his son, Jerry, and was decorated with flowers and peace symbols.

It was a bitterly cold December day in the kind of neighborhood where the city doesn't bother to clear the snow. People looked on silently from the windows of decaying buildings, and you could see the conditions that first provoked Phil's anger against the injustice of poverty in a nation of enormous wealth.

Some thousand people crowded into the church. A young priest, a friend of the Berrigans, dressed in white clerical robes, officiated. The service was suffused with religious solemnity—Buddhist chants, church hymns, prayers—and in the background the soft sounds of children, while all around were colorful posters and paintings: No More War, Peace Is the Way.

Phil's wife, Elizabeth McAlister, son Jerry, and daughters Frida and Kate spoke lovingly, eloquently, of their father. Daniel Berrigan, priest, poet, and brother, read one of his poems. Bread and wine were handed out.

Someone read the statement Phil dictated to Liz when he was unable to hold a pen. He spoke of his community in Jonah House in Baltimore. "They have always been a lifeline to me." He knew the end was near but was unwavering in his commitment: "I die with the conviction that nuclear weapons are the scourge of the Earth; to mine for them, manufacture them, deploy them, use them, is a curse against God, the human family, and the Earth itself."

Phil Berrigan was a hero in a time when we cannot find heroes among the politicians in Washington, much less the timorous press.

The real heroes are not on national television or in the headlines. They are the nurses, the doctors, the teachers, the social workers, the community organizers, the hospital orderlies, the construction workers, the people who keep the society going, who help people in need. They are the advocates for the homeless, the students asking a living wage for the campus janitors, the environmental activists trying to protect the trees, the air, the water. And they are the protesters against war, the apostles of peace in a world going mad with violence.

Among these was Philip Berrigan. Phil was a priest who defied his church by marrying his sweetheart, a former nun. He defied his government by challenging its accumulation of nuclear weapons, its death-dealing wars in Southeast Asia, Latin America, and the Middle East. And he went to prison again and again because he committed civil disobedience: pouring blood on nuclear warheads, hammering away at America's weapons of mass destruction.

He saw combat as an infantryman in World War II and came away from that war with the belief that war does not solve the fundamental problems that face the human race.

As a young Catholic priest, he worked among poor black people in Baltimore, and he became convinced that racism and poverty were intertwined. He was an early opponent of the war in Vietnam, and he believed, as Martin Luther King Jr. said, that "the evils of capitalism are as real as the evils of militarism and the evils of racism."

I came to know Phil Berrigan well, at first through his brother. Dan and I became good friends when we flew to Hanoi during the Tet Offensive of January 1968 to bring back three American airmen whom the North Vietnamese had decided to release from prison as a goodwill gesture for the Tet holiday.

It was shortly after our return that Dan joined his brother Phil and seven others in a dramatic protest against the war. They invaded the selective service office in Catonsville, Maryland, pulled draft files out of their cabinets, piled them outside, and set them afire with homemade napalm. The protesters, immediately arrested, became known as the Catonsville 9.

They were calling attention to the burned children of Vietnam, victims of the napalm dropped by American planes.

Dan Berrigan wrote, in advance of the Catonsville action: "Our apologies, good friends, for the fracture of good order, the burning of paper instead of children. How many must die before our voices are heard, how many must be tortured, dislocated, starved, maddened? When, at what point, will you say no to this war?"

They were convicted and sentenced to several years in jail. When their appeals were exhausted, Phil Berrigan and Dan Berrigan refused to give themselves up and went into hiding. They believed in continuing the civil disobedience they had begun.

It was at this point that I was invited to speak at an antiwar rally at a Catholic church on the Upper East Side of Manhattan. When I arrived, I found that the FBI had smashed its way into the priest's quarters, where Phil Berrigan was hiding, and had taken him into custody. Dan Berrigan remained underground for four months (during which time I and some friends helped him move about in the Boston area) before he was apprehended.

My wife, Roslyn, and I visited Phil and Dan as they were serving time in Danbury Prison. When they were released after several years, they continued to protest against the war in Vietnam. And when the war was over, Phil, Dan, Liz, and their community of religious pacifists did not stop.

In 1980, they carried out the first of what would be dozens of "Plowshares" actions, symbolic sabotage against nuclear weapons. There were many trials, many jail terms.

Altogether, Phil Berrigan served more than ten years in various prisons for his passionate insistence that war was a cruel response to the problems people faced in this country and around the globe.

It was not long after his release from his last prison sentence that he was diagnosed with kidney and liver cancer. Four months later, he died. To the end, he was nurtured by the community of men and women who lived together for years in Jonah House, sharing their possessions, caring for the children when the parents were in jail.

Philip Berrigan was imprisoned again and again because he wanted peace. He is gone now. But his struggle is carried on by Liz, by their three children, and by the extraordinary community of fellow lawbreakers in Jonah House and neighboring Viva House (holy outlaws, Dan Berrigan once called them).

Brendan Walsh and Willa Bickham at Viva House—former priest and former nun, now married—spoke at the funeral. Brendan said what everyone felt:

> Philip Berrigan is a friend to all the poor of Baltimore City. Philip Berrigan is a friend to all the people of the world who are bombed and scattered, who are starved, trampled upon, imprisoned, tortured, humiliated, scoffed at, dismissed as nobodies. He was that rare combination where word and deed were one. Always. Everywhere. Steadfast. Rock solid. Hopeful. One in a million. He was that tree standing by the water that would not be moved. Yes, Phil, *Deo gratias!* Thanks be to God! For your life. For your spirit that is still with us. Now, with you gone to another place, all of us will have to do more. *Couragio* to you, Phil!

Countless people all over the nation, and in other parts of the world, will remember Phil Berrigan as one of the heroes of our time—along with Gandhi, A. J. Muste, Dorothy Day, Martin Luther King Jr. They and so many others, not famous, who have struggled against war, who have tried to live the principles of a loving community, teach us what heroism is.

29

MISSISSIPPI FREEDOM SUMMER

S urely one of the great social movements in the history of the United States was that extraordinary burst of energy and courage that took place in the 1950s and 1960s in the South—the struggle for equal rights for African Americans. Its roots went far back to the antislavery movement in the decades before the Civil War, and to that brief period after the war when black people voted, held office, and demanded that promises of land and freedom made in the heat of the war be fulfilled.

Those promises—embodied in the Fourteenth and Fifteenth Amendments to the Constitution—were not kept, and there followed almost a hundred years of segregation, humiliation, brutality, poverty, and lynching, enforced by the states, with the tacit consent of the national government. In reaction to that terrible period, African Americans, their indignation long pent-up, rebelled all over the South, and changed not only that section of the country, but the consciousness of the nation itself.

The highlights of that story have been told many times— the Montgomery bus boycott, the sit-ins, the Freedom Rides, the street demonstrations in Birmingham, Alabama, the march from Selma to Montgomery—all of that agitation forcing the passage of the Civil Rights Act of 1964 and the Voting Rights Act of 1965. The heroes of that struggle have become known: Martin Luther King Jr., Rosa Parks, Fannie Lou Hamer, Stokely Carmichael.

However, the history of our country, as told in our textbooks, and in the culture at large, is mostly still confined to those highlights, still focused on certain important individuals. There are a thousand stories that are part of the larger one and that remain untold. There are countless individuals, anonymous, unheralded, whose commitment, whose bravery, have not been recognized.

Kathy Emery's *People Make Movements: Lessons from Freedom Summer*, forthcoming from Common Courage Press, is one of many attempts to recognize the untold history of that time, to tell, in this case, one important story: that of the Mississippi Freedom Summer of 1964, and the Freedom Schools that emerged during that summer. It is also an effort to bring to the forefront those unnamed individuals who played a crucial part in the struggles of that summer.

Doing that is a direct challenge, not only to the orthodox history of those years, but to the very idea of a history told from the point of view of the authorities—a history confined to "important" people that ignores the struggles of ordinary people. The orthodox approach perpetuates the idea that history is made from the top, and leaves to the mass of the people the most feeble of roles: that of voting every four years for a member of the Establishment chosen by the elite of the two major parties.

Recounting the history of the Mississippi Freedom Summer of 1964, and the extraordinary experience of the Freedom Schools, does more than suggest a different view of history. It presents a unique approach to education, one that is not the outcome of abstract theorizing, but that has been forged out of a rare educational experiment, carried out, unbelievably and yet necessarily, in the midst of an ongoing social struggle.

The Freedom Schools were a challenge not only to the social structure of Mississippi, but to American education as a whole. They began with the provocative suggestion that an entire school system can be created in a community outside the official order, and critical of its suppositions.

That experience, and Kathy Emery's book, ask questions which get at the heart of what education should be about. Can we, somehow, bring teachers and students together, not through the artificial sieve of certification and examination but on the basis of their common commitment to an exciting social goal? Can we solve the old educational problem of how to teach children crucial values, while avoiding a blanket imposition of the teacher's ideas?

Can we forthrightly accept as an educational goal that we want better human beings in the rising generation than we had in the last, and that this requires a bold declaration that the educational process cherishes equality, justice, compassion, and a global community? Is it possible to create a hunger for those goals through the fiercest argument about whether or not they are indeed worthwhile? And can the schools have a running, no-ideas-barred exchange of views about alternative ways to those goals?

Is there, in the war-torn, troubled atmosphere of our time, a national equivalent to the excitement of that great social movement of the Sixties? Can a new movement in our time be strong enough in its pull to create a motivation for learning that even the enticements of monetary success cannot match? Would it be possible to declare boldly that the aim of the schools is to find solutions for poverty, for injustice, for racial and national hatred, for violence and war? Can we turn all educational efforts into a national striving for those solutions?

There is certainly no point expecting the government to initiate such a questioning. Social movements like the one in the South came into being precisely because government ignored its charge, established in the Declaration of Independence, to assure for everyone an equal right to life, liberty, the pursuit of happiness. The people themselves will have to begin, perhaps to set up other pilot ventures, imperfect, but suggestive like that of the Mississippi Freedom Summer. Education can, and should, be dangerous to the existing social structure.

30

EUGENE V. DEBS

We are always in need of radicals who are also lovable, and so we would do well to remember Eugene Victor Debs. It was approximately 100 years ago that Debs was nationally famous as leader of the Socialist Party, and the poet James Whitcomb Riley wrote of him:

> *As warm a heart as ever beat*
> *Betwixt here and the Judgment Seat.*

Debs was what every socialist or anarchist or radical should be: fierce in his convictions, kind and compassionate in his personal relations. Sam Moore, a fellow inmate of the Atlanta penitentiary, where Debs was imprisoned for opposing the First World War, remembered how he felt as Debs was about to be released on Christmas Day, 1921: "As miserable as I was, I would defy fate with all its cruelty as long as Debs held my hand, and I was the most miserably happiest man on Earth when I knew he was going home Christmas."

Debs had won the hearts of his fellow prisoners in Atlanta. He had fought for them in a hundred ways and refused any special privileges for himself. On the day of his release, the warden ignored prison regulations and opened every cellblock to allow more than two thousand inmates to gather in front of the main jail building to say good-bye to Eugene Debs. As he started down the walkway from the prison, a roar went up and he turned, tears streaming down his face, and stretched out his arms to the other prisoners.

This was not his first prison experience. In 1894, not yet a socialist but an organizer for the American Railway Union, he had led a nationwide boycott of the railroads in support of the striking workers at the Pullman Palace Car Company. They tied up the railroad system, burned hundreds of railway cars, and were met with the full force of the capitalist state; Attorney General Richard Olney, a former railroad lawyer, got a court injunction to prohibit blocking trains. President Cleveland called out the army, which used bayonets and rifle fire on a crowd of five thousand strike sympathizers in Chicago. Seven hundred were arrested. Thirteen were shot to death.

Debs was jailed for violating a court injunction that prohibited him from aiding the strike in any way. In court, he denied he was a socialist, but during his six months in prison he read socialist literature, and the events of the strike took on a deeper meaning. He wrote later: "I was to be baptized in socialism in the roar of conflict. . . . In the gleam of every bayonet and the flash of every rifle the class struggle was revealed."

From then on, Debs devoted his life to the cause of working people and the dream of a socialist society. In 1905 he stood on the platform with Mother Jones and Big Bill Haywood at the founding convention of the Industrial Workers of the World. He was a magnificent speaker, his long body leaning forward from the podium, his arm raised dramatically. Thousands came to hear him talk all over the country.

With the outbreak of war in Europe in 1914 and the buildup of war fever against Germany, some socialists succumbed to the talk of "preparedness," but Debs was adamantly opposed. When President Wilson and Congress brought the nation into the war in 1917, speech was no longer free. The Espionage Act made it a crime to say anything that would discourage enlistment in the armed forces. Soon, close to a thousand people were in prison for protesting the war.

Debs made a speech in Canton, Ohio, in support of the men and women in jail for opposing the war. He told his listeners: "Wars throughout history have been waged for conquest and plunder. . . . And that is war, in a nutshell. The master class has always declared the wars; the subject class has always fought the battles." He was found guilty and sentenced to ten years in prison by a judge who denounced those "who would strike the sword from the hand of this nation while she is engaged in defending herself against a foreign and brutal power."

In court, Debs refused to call any witnesses, declaring: "I have been accused of obstructing the war. I admit it. I abhor war. I would oppose war if I stood alone." Before sentencing, Debs spoke to judge and jury, uttering perhaps his most famous words. I was in his hometown of Terre Haute, Indiana, recently, among two hundred people gathered to honor his memory, and we began the evening by reciting those words—words that moved me deeply when I first read them and move me deeply still: "While there is a lower class, I am in it. While there is a criminal element, I am of it. While there is a soul in prison, I am not free."

The "liberal" Oliver Wendell Holmes, speaking for a unanimous Supreme Court, upheld the verdict, on the ground that Debs's speech was intended to obstruct military recruiting. When the war was over, President Woodrow Wilson turned down his attorney general's recommendation that Debs be released, even though he was sixty-five and in poor health. Debs was in prison for thirty-two months. Finally, in 1921, the Republican Warren Harding ordered him freed on Christmas Day.

Today, as capitalism, "the free market," and "private enterprise" are being hailed as triumphant in the world, it is a good time to remember Debs and to rekindle the idea of socialism.

To see the disintegration of the Soviet Union as a sign of the failure of socialism is to mistake the monstrous tyranny created by Stalin for the vision of an egalitarian and democratic society that has inspired enormous numbers of people all over the world. Indeed, the removal of the Soviet Union as the false surrogate for the idea of socialism creates a great opportunity. We can now reintroduce genuine socialism to a world feeling the sickness of capitalism: its nationalist hatreds, its perpetual warfare, riches for a small number of people in a small number of countries, and hunger, homelessness, and insecurity for everyone else.

Here in the United States we should recall that enthusiasm for socialism—production for use instead of profit, economic and social equality, solidarity with our brothers and sisters all over the world—was at its height before the Soviet Union came into being.

In the era of Debs, the first seventeen years of the twentieth century—until war created an opportunity to crush the movement—millions of Americans declared their adherence to the principles of socialism. Those were years of bitter labor struggles, the great walkouts of women garment workers in New York, the victorious multiethnic strike of textile workers in Lawrence, Massachusetts, the unbelievable courage of coal miners in Colorado, defying the power and wealth of the Rockefellers. The Wobblies were born—revolutionary, militant, demanding "one big union" for everyone, skilled and unskilled, black and white, men and women, native-born and foreign-born.

More than a million people read *Appeal to Reason* and other socialist newspapers. In proportion to the population, it would be as if today more than 3 million Americans read a socialist press. The party had 100,000 members, and 1,200 officeholders in 340 municipalities. Socialism was especially strong in the Southwest, among tenant farmers, railroad workers, coal miners, lumberjacks. Oklahoma had 12,000 dues-paying members in 1914 and more than 100 socialists in local offices. It was the home of the fiery Kate Richards O'Hare. Jailed for opposing the war, she once hurled a book through a skylight to bring fresh air into the foul-smelling jail block, bringing cheers from her fellow inmates.

The point of recalling all this is to remind us of the powerful appeal of the socialist idea to people alienated from the political system—as so many are today—and to increase awareness of the growing disparities in income and wealth. The word itself—"socialism"—may still carry the burden of having been distorted by the Soviet Union and other despotisms. But anyone who goes around the country, or reads carefully the public opinion surveys over the past decade, can see that huge numbers of Americans agree on what should be the fundamental elements of a decent society: guaranteed food, housing, medical care for everyone; democratic control of corporate power; equal rights for all races, genders, and sexual orientations; a recognition of the rights of immigrants as the unrecognized counterparts of our parents and grandparents; the rejection of the death penalty, war, and violence as solutions for crime, tyranny, and injustice.

There are people fearful of the word, all along the political spectrum. What is important, I think, is not the word, but a determination to hold up before a troubled public those ideas that are both bold and inviting—the more bold, the more inviting. That's what remembering Debs and the socialist idea can do for us.

31

PROTEST LITERATURE

I was reading "protest literature" as a teenager—Charles Dickens's *Hard Times*, John Steinbeck's *The Grapes of Wrath*, Upton Sinclair's *Boston*—without distinguishing it from any other kind of literature. But there was clearly something about this kind of writing that held a special attraction for me. Only later did I realize that even the aesthetic element in such literature (which is all, some people think, one should care about) was enhanced for me by the fact that it was a political act thrust into the social struggles of our time.

How, exactly—or even roughly—does protest literature do what I assume it is meant to do: change the world? Or, more modestly, to enhance the social consciousness of a reader, moving him or her to think about injustice and even to act against it?

I can think of several ways in which such writing has the effect I am talking about. And I must add that I am not distinguishing between fiction and nonfiction, not just because you find protest literature in both, but also because the line between the two is not clear, as fiction may give you powerful factual information, and nonfiction is in its own way an imaginative reconstruction of reality.

The most obvious—and therefore often overlooked—contribution to social change that literature can make is simply to inform people of something they know nothing about, to startle them with new information into thinking of something that was outside their vision or their knowledge. When Upton Sinclair wrote *The Jungle*, what he told about the meatpacking industry—both the conditions of the people who worked there and the quality of meat that made its way into kitchens all over America—provoked such concern as to cause Congress to pass the Meat Inspection Act of 1906. Rachel Carson's *The Sea Around Us* and *Silent Spring* led millions of people to think, for the first time, about their natural environment and sparked not only national legislation but the beginning of a social movement.

There are other situations where we believe we know something but don't really know it in a visceral way, don't really know it emotionally, to the point where it moves us to action. White people in the United States always "knew" that black people were discriminated against. Certainly that was true of the white students in my classes at Boston University. But it was only when they read Malcolm X's *Autobiography* or Richard Wright's *Black Boy* or the poems of Countee Cullen and Langston Hughes that they were confronted by the reality of the lives of black people. They had no idea why black people might be so angry and so were not only confused but also afraid of that anger. The prose of Malcolm X, of James Baldwin, could make them, for the first time, feel and understand that anger.

I knew, as a young man, or thought I knew, that black people were treated as inferiors, discriminated against in a hundred ways. One day I picked up a book of poems by Countee Cullen, poet of the Harlem Renaissance, and read a poem called "Incident." In it, he recalls a trip to Baltimore, eight-years-old, sitting on a bus, when a white boy, about his own age, stuck out his tongue and called him "nigger." The poem's last lines are: "I traveled all through Baltimore, from May until December, but of all the things that happened there, that's all that I remember." Those lines reached deep inside me, for the first time making me understand what it must be like to feel humiliated because of your color. After all, humiliation, aside from color or any other trivial human characteristic, is a universal experience.

Here's another example of what I mean by really, really knowing something. Everyone knows war is hell. But unless you have been inside a war, it remains an abstraction, the numbers of the dead just numbers, the crosses in the cemetery just crosses. But there is a literature of war that brings you up short, makes you think for the first time about what it's truly, truly like, in such a way as to revolt you, nauseate you, and turn you against war no matter what lofty justifications come out of the mouths of Authority.

That was the effect that, as a young man, reading Dalton Trumbo's novel *Johnny Got His Gun* had on me. Here was war, brought home to me in a way I had never experienced. The stump of a young American is found in the no-man's-land of the First World War. It is a torso without arms or legs, unable to see or hear, but the heart is still beating and the brain is still working. It is brought onto a hospital bed, and the novel consists of the thoughts going on in that brain, and the struggle, finally successful, to communicate with the outside world. Generals arrive to pin a medal on his chest. They ask him: "What do you want?"

The response: "Take me into the schoolhouses all the schoolhouses in the world. . . . Take me wherever there are parliaments and diets and congresses and chambers of statesmen. I want to be there when they talk about honor and justice and making the world safe for democracy and four-teen points and the self-determination of people. . . . But before they vote on them before they give the order for all the little guys to start killing each other let the main guy rap his gavel on my case and point down at me and say here gen-tlemen is the only issue before this house and that is are you for this thing here or are you against it."

As I've mentioned, I was in a war, bombing cities in Europe during World War II. And yet, I didn't really under-stand what I was doing, what was happening to the human beings below. Flying miles above the ground, releasing my bombs, I could hear no screams, see no blood, no mangled corpses of children. Modern warfare can remove even com-batants from the human effects of their actions. I reacted to the bombing of Hiroshima as I had reacted to my own bombing missions, with a coldness I am still ashamed of.

There is still another way in which literature can affect our social consciousness: by creating bizarre and unreal situations which upset our ways of thinking about the world by going outside the boundaries of "rational" thought, thus com-pelling us to make a radical break from the orthodoxies that confine us. Yes, the literature of the absurd.

I think of Voltaire's *Candide*; how many thousands of ser-mons are preached every Sunday where in the midst of a world in pain we are assured by the Pangloss in the pulpit that it is God's will.

I think of Joseph Heller's *Catch-22* and the scene in the Italian brothel where an old man says to the American flier Yossarian something like this: "We Italians, we will win, because we are so weak. You Americans will lose because you are so strong."

An absurd statement, but if you don't immediately dismiss those words, they may haunt you and make you think in ways you haven't thought before, as the *Tao Te Ching* does in its own way.

Ultimately, protest literature should move people to think more broadly, to feel more deeply, begin to act, perhaps alone at first, but then with others, on the supposition that social change comes about through the combined and cumulative actions of many people, even if they do not know one another or are not aware of the other's existence. If this is so, then Kurt Vonnegut's comment in *Timequake* is appropriate. He has been asked many times, he says, about why he bothers writing. He responds that he writes so that the reader knows that "I care about the same things you care about. You are not alone."

If protest literature does nothing but that, it has done something profoundly important.

32

FILM AND HISTORY

Like so many World War II veterans (I could see them all around me in the cinema's audience), I was drawn to see *Saving Private Ryan*. I had volunteered for the Air Force at the age of twenty, trained as a bombardier, and flew some of the last bombing missions of the European war.

My pilot was nineteen. My tailgunner was eighteen. Every death in *Saving Private Ryan* reminded me, as it must have reminded other veterans, of how lucky we were, we who survived. My two closest air force buddies who went through training with me and then went on to other theaters (what a word, "theaters"!)—Joe Perry to Italy, Ed Plotkin to the Pacific—were killed in the last weeks of the war.

I watched *Private Ryan*'s extraordinarily photographed battle scenes, and I was thoroughly taken in. But when the movie was over, I realized that it was exactly that—*I had been taken in*. And I disliked the film intensely. I was angry at it because I did not want the suffering of men in war to be used—yes, *exploited*—in such a way as to revive what should be buried along with all those bodies in Arlington Cemetery: the glory of military heroism.

"The greatest war movie ever made," the film critics wrote about *Saving Private Ryan*. They are a disappointing lot, the film critics. They are excited, even exultant, about the brilliant cinematography, depicting the bloody chaos of the Omaha Beach landing. But they are pitifully superficial.

They fail, with a few honorable exceptions (such as Vincent Canby in the *New York Times* and Donald Murray in the *Boston Globe*) to ask the most important question: will this film help persuade the next generation that such scenes must never occur again?

The admiring critics of the movie gave their own answer to that; it is a war movie, they say, not an antiwar movie.

Some viewers have asked how can anyone want to go to war after seeing such horror? But knowing the horrors of war has never been an obstacle to a quick buildup of war spirit by patriotic political speeches and an obsequious press.

All that bloodshed, all that pain, all those severed limbs and exposed intestines will not deter a brave people from going to war. They just need to believe that the cause is just.

In *Saving Private Ryan*, there is never any doubt that the cause is just. There is no need to say the words explicitly. The heartrending crosses in Arlington National Cemetery get the message across, loud and clear. And a benign General Marshall, front and back of the movie, quotes Abraham Lincoln's words of solace to a mother who has lost five sons in the Civil War. The audience is left with no choice but to conclude that this one—while it causes sorrow to a million mothers—is waged for a good cause.

Saving Private Ryan, aided by superb cinematographic technology, draws on our deep feeling for the GIs in order to rescue not just Private Ryan but the good name of war.

The film was nominated for eleven Academy Awards, and won five. But then again, didn't Kissinger get a Nobel Prize? The committees that give prizes are, too often, bereft of social conscience. But we are not bound to honor their choices.

To refresh my memory, I watched the video of *All Quiet on the Western Front*. With no musical background, without the benefit of modern cinematography, without fields of corpses, with no pools of blood reddening the screen, that film conveys the horror of warfare more powerfully than *Saving Private Ryan*. The one fleeting shot of two hands clutching barbed wire, the rest of the body gone, says it all.

In Spielberg's film, we see Tom Hanks gunned down, and it is sad. But it is a prosaic sadness compared to the death of the protagonist in Erich Remarque's story, as we watch a butterfly hover over a trench, and we see the hand of Lew Ayres reach out for it and go limp. We see no dead body, only that beautiful butterfly, and the reaching hand.

But more important, *All Quiet on the Western Front* does not dodge—as *Saving Private Ryan* and its gushing critics do—the issue of war. In it, war is not just horrible; it is futile. It is not inevitable; it is manufactured. Back home, commenting on the war, is no kindly General Marshall, quoting Lincoln, but prosperous men urging the soldiers, "On to Paris, boys! On to Paris!"

The boys in the trenches don't just discuss the battle; they discuss the war. They ask: who is profiting? They propose: hey, let's have the world's leaders get into an arena and fight it out themselves! They acknowledge: we have no quarrel with the boys on the other side of the barbed wire!

Our culture is in deep trouble when a film like *Saving Private Ryan* can pass by, like a military parade, with nothing but a shower of confetti and hurrahs for its color and grandeur.

Do narrative films or documentaries treat historical subjects better? I don't think there is a clear-cut answer. Sometimes a narrative does it better, sometimes a documentary. In short, there are good and bad narratives, good and bad documentaries.

By "good" I am not talking about being true to historical detail. The details might be true or invented, but whether a historical film is "good" depends on whether the film as a whole conveys an important idea with power and artistry. One might think that documentaries must naturally be more true to the history of an event or a period, but they are as subject to distortion as narrative films. That is so because any history is a selection of data from an enormous base, with the historian (or filmmaker) deciding what to include and what to omit. Therefore "nonfiction" can be as fictional or more fictional than fiction.

You can have several different historical accounts in a documentary, all "true" in the sense that everything put on screen really happened, but important information has been omitted that would change the effect of the presentation. For instance you can tell the story of Columbus, his plans for his voyage, the voyage itself, his navigational skills, his courage. But if you omit the mutilation, kidnapping, and killing of the American Indians he encountered, a false impression has been left. You could do a fictional account of the Columbus story that would be more "true" to the reality of his encounter with the American Indians.

All of this is to say that a film is not inherently "true" because it is a documentary. Similarly, a fictional account, a narrative, which invents certain details and even characters, may be more "true" to the historical event than the documentary.

There are also limitations of narrative treatments. In dramatizing an event, there is the temptation to overwhelm the history with a personal story. It may well be that the film *Reds*, which was a pioneering film in dealing with the difficult and controversial story of an American Communist in relation to the Bolshevik Revolution, allowed the history to be obscured by the love story of John Reed and Louise Bryant.

A documentary need not yield dramatic impact to a story, if it's well done. The documentary *Eyes on the Prize* treated the Southern sit-ins of 1960 in an emotionally charged and dramatic way that would be hard for a narrative film to equal. Ken Burns's documentary on the Civil War, on the other hand, was technically very well done, but it was a military history with so much emphasis on the famous battles of the war that the politics and economics of the war got short shrift. The end result was to repeat the orthodox history, though visually with great drama.

A documentary can be quantitatively superior, that is, tell more of a historical story than a narrative, which by its nature focuses on one person's story or one event to represent an epoch. Yet the narrative, despite that limitation, may be better qualitatively, in the sense of bringing the viewer emotionally and intellectually into the event. I think of the film *The Grapes of Wrath* as bringing the viewer into the Depression of the 1930s more effectively than a documentary about "the Depression era" might do, even with moving footage of people out of work, being evicted from their tenements, riding the rails. Or perhaps we should say that, in this case (I think of the fine documentary *Riding the Rails*) both narrative and documentary can do good a job in different ways.

Similarly, the narrative film *Norma Rae* and the documentary *Union Maids* both effectively give a picture of working people being organized into unions and going on strike.

The film *Paths of Glory* depicts the horrors of war in a context where the lives of soldiers are sacrificed for the avarice and ambition of politicians, industrialists, and generals. It is hard to imagine a documentary on World War I that would convey those ideas as powerfully. *Catch-22*, based on Joseph Heller's novel, did not fill the screen with bloody battle scenes a la Spielberg, but managed to convey a different kind of horror: that young men were risking their lives on behalf of fools in high places and that cities were being bombed without reason.

In my classes, I would use both documentaries and feature films, depending on which I thought would more effectively make the point I was trying to get across to my students. I showed them the documentary *Attica* to convey the fascistic nature of prisons and the willingness of political leaders to sacrifice innocent people (the guards as well as the prisoners) to make a point. This was a parable about war, as well as a film about prisons. It would be hard to find a feature film that would make that point as powerfully, although movies like *The Shawshank Redemption* do give viewers an idea of the hell of prison life.

I also showed the film *Burn*, probably the only Marlon Brando film that was buried by its distributor. When I called United Artists to ask how I could get a copy for my class, the person at the other end said they had withdrawn it from circulation. When I asked why he began shouting "Because it's an obscene, dirty film." I found that very funny (in both senses of the word) because there was no sex in *Burn* and United Artists at that time was ballyhooing another Brando film, *Last Tango in Paris*. This suggested that the "obscenity" had to do with the fact that *Burn* was about colonialism, and the way one colonial power, England, evicted another, Portugal, from a desirable colony, pretending to bring freedom to the native population. If shown today, the film might well be instructive about "Operation Iraqi Freedom."

33

IMMIGRATION NATION

There is a simmering controversy in the United States about the status of our immigrants. There are loud cries from nationalist ideologues, but also from ordinary citizens who feel threatened by the influx of non-English-speaking people, especially from Mexico. Armed vigilantes patrol the borders looking for those who might cross over, and the president of the United States has deployed thousands of National Guardsmen to the border to do the same.

Roused by the increasing hostility, immigrants and their advocates all over the country—especially in border states like California and Arizona—have been demonstrating by the hundreds of thousands for the rights of foreign-born people, whether here legally or illegally. One sign is seen in every demonstration: "No Human Being Is Illegal."

At the same time, members of Congress, conscious of their political fortunes, are trying to both assuage the anti-immigrant feelings of many of their constituents and meet the needs of employers who profit from cheap labor. As Congress debates legislation to deal with the situation, the members want to make some show of adherence to the ideal of generosity toward the foreign-born.

Discrimination against the foreign-born, often to the point of hatred, has a long history, going back to the beginning of the nation.

In the late eighteenth century, the United States, having just gone through its own revolution, was ironically fearful of having revolutionaries in its midst. The French had recently overthrown its monarchy, Irish rebels were protesting against British rule, and the new U.S. government was conscious of "dangerous foreigners"—Irish and French—in the country. In the year 1798, in a climate of "cold war" with France, Congress passed legislation lengthening the residence requirement for becoming a citizen from five to fourteen years. It also authorized the president to deport any alien he regarded as dangerous to public safety.

There was virulent anti-Irish sentiment in the 1840s and 1850s, especially after the failure of the potato crop in Ireland killed one million people and drove millions more abroad, most of them to the United States. "No Irish Need Apply," a phrase that often appeared in employment ads, symbolized the prejudice that existed against Irish immigrants. It was part of a long tradition of irrational fear in which one generation of immigrants, once partly assimilated, reacted with hatred to the next generation of immigrants. The Irish-born Dennis Kearney, for example, became a spokesman for anti-Chinese prejudice. His political ambitions led him and the California Workingmen's Party to adopt the slogan "The Chinese Must Go."

In the 1860s the Chinese had been welcome as cheap labor for the building of the transcontinental railroad. A decade later, especially after the economic crisis of 1873, hard-pressed white workers saw the Chinese as taking away jobs from the native-born. Industrialists no longer needed them for railroad work, and politicians saw them as useful scapegoats to explain the economic distress of white workers. It was not surprising, therefore, that Congress passed the Chinese Exclusion Act of 1882, which for the first time in the nation's history created the category of "illegal" immigrants. Chinese, desperate to find a better life in the United States, tried to evade the act by crossing into the United States from Mexico. Some learned to say *Yo soy Mexicano*, Spanish for *I am Mexican*. But violence against them continued, as whites, seeing their jobs go to ill-paid Chinese, reacted with fury. In Rock Springs, Wyoming, in the summer of 1885, whites attacked 500 Chinese miners, massacring 28 of them in cold blood.

Europeans, on the other hand, were welcome, especially on the East Coast, where they were needed as laborers, stonecutters, ditch diggers, or workers in garment factories, textile mills, and mines. The immigrants poured in from southern and eastern Europe, from Italy, Greece, Poland, Russia, and the Balkans. There were five million immigrants in the 1880s, four million in the 1890s. From 1900 to 1910, eight million more arrived.

Newcomers faced vicious hostility. Here is a typical comment from the *Baltimore Sun*: "The Italian immigrant would be no more objectionable than some others were it not for his singularly bloodthirsty disposition and frightful temper and vindictiveness." New York City's police commissioner, Theodore Bingham, insisted that "half of the criminals" in New York City in 1908 were Jews.

As mentioned earlier, there was widespread opposition when the United States entered World War I. To suppress the anti-war sentiment, the government adopted legislation—the Espionage Act and the Sedition Act—which led to the imprisonment of almost a thousand people. Their crime was to protest, by speech or writing, the United States' entrance into the war. Another law provided for the deportation of aliens who opposed organized government or advocated the destruction of property.

After the war, the lingering superpatriotic atmosphere led to more hysteria against the foreign born, intensified by the Bolshevik Revolution of 1917. In 1919, after the explosion of a bomb in front of the house of Attorney General A. Mitchell Palmer, a series of raids were carried out against immigrants. Palmer's agents picked up 249 noncitizens of Russian birth, many of whom had lived in this country a long time. They were put on a ship and deported to Soviet Russia. Anarchists Emma Goldman and Alexander Berkman were among those deported. J. Edgar Hoover, at that time a young agent of the Department of Justice, personally supervised the deportation.

Shortly after the Palmer raids, in January 1920, four thousand people in thirty-three cities were rounded up and detained in seclusion for long periods of time. They were subjected to secret hearings, and more than five hundred of them were deported. In Boston, Department of Justice agents, aided by local police, arrested six hundred people by raiding meeting halls and by invading private homes in the early morning. The people were handcuffed, chained together, and marched through the city streets. It was in this atmosphere of jingoism and antiforeign hysteria that the Italian immigrants Nicola Sacco and Bartolomeo Vanzetti were put on a trial after a robbery and murder at a Massachusetts shoe factory, found guilty by an Anglo-Saxon judge and jury, and sentenced to death.

The rise in nationalist and antiforeign sentiment during World War I led to the passage of the National Origins Quota Act in 1924. The act set quotas that encouraged immigration from England, Germany, and Scandinavia and strictly limited immigration from eastern and southern Europe.

Following World War II, the Cold War atmosphere of anti-Communist hysteria brought about the McCarran-Walter Act of 1952. The act permitted immigrants from the United Kingdom, Ireland, and Germany to fill 70 percent of the total annual immigration quota but set quotas of a hundred immigrants for each country in Asia. The act also revived, in a particularly virulent way, the anti-alien legislation of 1798, creating ideological grounds for the exclusion of immigrants and the treatment of all foreign-born residents, who could be deported for any "activities prejudicial to the public interest" or "subversive to national security." Noncitizens suspected of radical ideas were rounded up and deported.

The great social movements of the Sixties led to a number of legislative reforms, including voting rights for African Americans and health care for senior citizens and for the poor. Among these was a law abolishing the National Origins Quota system and allowing a maximum of twenty thousand immigrants to enter the United States from *each* country.

Although the Cold War presumably ended with the disintegration of the Soviet Union, the atmosphere of militarism and war continued. Panama was invaded in 1989 and Iraq in 1991.

When the Federal Building in Oklahoma City was bombed in 1995, killing 168 people, the two men convicted of the crime were native-born Americans. Nevertheless, the following year President Bill Clinton signed into law the Antiterrorism and Effective Death Penalty Act, which contained especially harsh provisions for foreign-born people. For immigrants as well as for citizens, the act reintroduced the McCarthy-era principle of "guilt by association." That is, people could be put in jail or, if foreign-born, deported, not for what they actually did, but for lending support to any group that the secretary of state designated as "terrorist." Visas could also be denied to people wanting to enter the United States if they were members of any such group, even if the actions of the group supported by the individual were perfectly legal. Under the new law, a person marked for deportation had no rights of due process and could be deported on the basis of secret evidence.

Clinton's signing of this act sent a clear message: targeting immigrants, and depriving them of constitutional rights, were not only characteristic of Republican right-wingers, but also of the Democratic Party, which in the military atmosphere of World War II and the Cold War, had joined a bipartisan attack on the rights of both the native- and foreign-born.

The attacks on 9/11 and George Bush's "war on terror" have created an anxious climate in which any foreign-born person is potentially an object of suspicion. Passage of the USA PATRIOT Act of 2001 gave the attorney general the power to detain any foreign-born person he declares a suspected terrorist. He doesn't need to show proof; he merely needs to say the word. The act established that any such detained persons may be held indefinitely, with no burden of proof on the government and no hearing required. The act was passed with both Democratic and Republican support; only Senator Russ Feingold (D-Wisconsin) voted against it.

In the tense atmosphere created by 9/11 and the war on terror, there were, predictably, numerous cases of violence against foreign-born people. For instance, just four days after the 9/11, a forty-nine-year-old Sikh American who was doing landscaping work outside his gas station in Mesa, Arizona, was shot and killed by a man shouting, "I stand for America all the way." In February 2003, a group of teenagers in Orange County, California, used bats and golf clubs to attack Rashid Alam, an eighteen-year-old Lebanese American. He suffered a broken jaw, stab wounds, and head injuries.

Shortly after 9/11, as documented by the Center for Constitutional Rights and Human Rights Watch, Muslims from various countries were picked up, held for various periods of time in tiny, windowless cells, and often beaten and abused. As the *New York Times* has since confirmed, "hundreds of Muslim immigrants . . . were swept up in the weeks after the 2001 terror attacks and held for months before they were cleared of links to terrorism and deported."

Incidents continue to occur. For instance, according to a report by the Meiklejohn Civil Liberties Institute, on October 23, 2003, federal agents raided sixty Wal-Mart stores in twenty-one states across the country and arrested 250 janitors employed by Wal-Mart contractors for alleged violations of immigration law. In a series of raids that began on May 26, 2006, swarms of federal agents arrested more than two thousand immigrants across the country.

Muslims have become a special target of surveillance and arrest. Thousands have been detained since 9/11. *New York Times* columnist Anthony Lewis told of one man, who, even before 9/11, was arrested on secret evidence. When a federal judge found there was no reason to conclude the man was a threat to national security, the man was released. However, after September 11, 2001, the Department of Justice, ignoring the judge's finding, imprisoned him again, and held him in solitary confinement twenty-three hours a day without allowing his family to see him.

Since the passage of the Antiterrorism and Effective Death Penalty Act of 1996, 1.5 million people have been deported from the United States. And after the immigration protests of May 2006, U.S. authorities have stepped up their raids, arrests, and deportations. What have been missing in so much of the debate about the rights of immigrants are the voices and the experiences of the immigrants themselves. Deepa Fernandes's gripping book, *Targeted*, is one of the few to present such voices.

As of summer 2006, Republicans and Democrats were attempting to arrive at a "compromise" on the rights of immigrants. But in none of their proposals is there a recognition that immigrants deserve the same rights as everyone else. Forgetting, or rather, ignoring the indignation of liberty-loving people at the building of the Berlin Wall, and the exultation that greeted its fall, there will be a wall built at the southern borders of California and Arizona. I doubt that any national political figure will point out that this wall is intended to keep Mexicans out of the land that was violently taken from Mexico in the Mexican War of 1846–48.

Only demonstrators in cities across the country are reminding us of the words on the Statue of Liberty in New York harbor:

> *"Give me your tired, your poor,*
> *Your huddled masses yearning to breathe free,*
> *The wretched refuse of your teeming shore.*
> *Send these, the homeless, tempest-tossed to me:*
> *I lift my lamp beside the golden door!"*

In the wave of anger against government action in the Sixties, cartoons were drawn showing the Statue of Liberty blindfolded. The blindfolds remain, if only symbolically, until we begin to act as if—yes—*no human being is illegal.*

34

SACCO AND VANZETTI

Fifty years after the executions of Italian immigrants Sacco and Vanzetti, Governor Michael S. Dukakis of Massachusetts set up a panel to judge the fairness of the trial, and the conclusion was that the two men had not received a fair trial. This aroused a minor storm in Boston. One letter, signed John M. Cabot, U.S. Ambassador Retired, declared his "great indignation" and pointed out that Governor Fuller's affirmation of the death sentence was made after a special review by "three of Massachusetts' most distinguished and respected citizens—President Lowell of Harvard, President Stratton of MIT and retired Judge Grant."

Those three "distinguished and respected citizens" were viewed differently by Heywood Broun, who wrote in his column for the *New York World* immediately after the governor's panel made its report. He wrote:

> It is not every prisoner who has a President of Harvard University throw on the switch for him. . . . If this is a lynching, at least the fish peddler and his friend the factory hand may take unction to their souls that they will die at the hands of men in dinner jackets or academic gowns.

Heywood Broun, one of the most distinguished journalists of the twentieth century, did not last long as a columnist for the *New York World*.

On that fiftieth year after the execution, the *New York Times* reported, "Plans by Mayor Beame to proclaim next Tuesday 'Sacco and Vanzetti Day' have been canceled in an effort to avoid controversy, a City Hall spokesman said yesterday."

There must be good reason why a case fifty years old, now over seventy-five years old, arouses such emotion. I suggest that it is because to talk about Sacco and Vanzetti inevitably brings up matters that trouble us today: our system of justice, the relationship between war fever and civil liberties, and most troubling of all, the ideas of anarchism: the obliteration of national boundaries and therefore of war, the elimination of poverty, and the creation of a full democracy.

The case of Sacco and Vanzetti revealed, in its starkest terms, that the noble words inscribed above our courthouses, "Equal Justice Before the Law," have always been a lie. Those two men, the fish peddler and the shoemaker, could not get justice in the American system, because justice is not meted out equally to the poor and the rich, the native-born and the foreign-born, the orthodox and the radical, the white and the person of color. And while injustice may play itself out today more subtly and in more intricate ways than it did in the crude circumstances of the Sacco and Vanzetti case, its essence remains.

In their case, the unfairness was flagrant. They were being tried for robbery and murder, but in the minds, and in the behavior of the prosecuting attorney, the judge, and the jury, the important thing about them was that they were, as Upton Sinclair put it in his remarkable novel *Boston*, "wops," foreigners, poor workingmen, radicals.

Here is a sample of the police interrogation:

POLICE: Are you a citizen?
SACCO: No.
POLICE: Are you a Communist?
SACCO: No.
POLICE: Anarchist?
SACCO: No.
POLICE: Do you believe in this government of ours?
SACCO: Yes; some things I like different.

What did these questions have to do with the robbery of a shoe factory in South Braintree, Massachusetts, and the shooting of a paymaster and a guard?

Sacco was lying, of course. *No, I'm not a Communist. No, I'm not an anarchist.* Why would he lie to the police? Why would a Jew lie to the Gestapo? Why would a black in South Africa lie to his interrogators? Why would a dissident in Soviet Russia lie to the secret police? Because they all know there is no justice for them.

Has there ever been justice in the American system for the poor, the person of color, the radical? When the eight anarchists of Chicago were sentenced to death after the Haymarket riot (a police riot, that is) of 1886, it was not because there was any proof of a connection between them and the bomb thrown in the midst of the police; there was not a shred of evidence. It was because they were leaders of the anarchist movement in Chicago.

When Eugene Debs and a thousand others were sent to prison during World War I, under the Espionage Act, was it because they were guilty of espionage? Hardly. They were socialists who spoke out against the war. In affirming the ten-year sentence of Debs, Supreme Court Justice Oliver Wendell Holmes made it clear why Debs must go to prison. He quoted from Debs's speech: "The master class has always declared the wars, the subject class has always fought the battles."

Holmes, much admired as one of our great liberal jurists, made clear the limits of liberalism, its boundaries set by a vindictive nationalism. After all the appeals of Sacco and Vanzetti had been exhausted, the case was put before Holmes, sitting on the Supreme Court. He refused to review the case, thus letting the verdict stand.

In our time, Ethel and Julius Rosenberg were sent to the electric chair. Was it because they were guilty beyond a reasonable doubt of passing atomic secrets to the Soviet Union? Or was it because they were Communists, as the prosecutor made clear, with the approval of the judge? Was it also because the country was in the midst of anti-Communist hysteria, Communists had just taken power in China, there was a war in Korea, and the weight of all that could be borne by two American Communists?

Why was George Jackson, in California, sentenced to ten years in prison for a $70 robbery, and then shot to death by guards? Was it because he was poor, black, and radical?

Can a Muslim today, in the atmosphere of the "war on terror" be given equal justice before the law? Why was my upstairs neighbor, a dark-skinned Brazilian who might look like a Middle East Muslim, pulled out of his car by police, though he had violated no regulation, and questioned and humiliated?

Why are the 2 million people in American jails and prisons, and 6 million people under parole, probation, or surveillance, disproportionately people of color, disproportionately poor? A study showed that 70 percent of the people in New York State prisons came from seven neighborhoods in New York City—neighborhoods of poverty and desperation.

Class injustice cuts across every decade, every century of our history. In the midst of the Sacco and Vanzetti case, a wealthy man in the town of Milton, south of Boston, shot and killed a man who was gathering firewood on his property. He spent eight days in jail, then was let out on bail, and was not prosecuted. The district attorney called it "justifiable homicide." One law for the rich, one law for the poor—a persistent characteristic of our system of justice.

But being poor was not the chief crime of Sacco and Vanzetti. They were Italians, immigrants, anarchists. It was less than two years from the end of the First World War. They had protested against the war. They had refused to be drafted. They saw hysteria mount against radicals and foreigners, observed the raids carried out by Attorney General Palmer's agents in the Department of Justice, who broke into homes in the middle of the night without warrants, held people incommunicado, and beat them with clubs and blackjacks.

In Boston, five hundred people were arrested, chained together, and marched through the streets. Luigi Galleani, editor of the anarchist paper *Cronaca Sovversiva*, to which Sacco and Vanzetti subscribed, was picked up in Boston and quickly deported.

Something even more frightening had happened. A fellow anarchist of Sacco and Vanzetti, a typesetter named Andrea Salsedo, who lived in New York, was kidnapped by members of the Federal Bureau of Investigation (I use the word "kidnapped" to describe an illegal seizure of a person) and held in FBI offices on the fourteenth floor of the Park Row Building. He was not allowed to call his family, friends, or a lawyer, and was questioned and beaten, according to a fellow prisoner. During the eighth week of his imprisonment, on May 3, 1920, the body of Salsedo, smashed to a pulp, was found on the pavement near the Park Row Building, and the FBI announced that he had committed suicide by jumping from the fourteenth floor window of the room in which they had kept him. This was just two days before Sacco and Vanzetti were arrested.

We know today, as a result of congressional reports in 1975, of the FBI's COINTELPRO program in which FBI agents broke into people's homes and offices, carried out illegal wiretaps, were involved in acts of violence to the point of murder, and collaborated with the Chicago police in the killing of two Black Panther leaders in 1969. The FBI and the CIA have violated the law again and again. There is no punishment for them.

There has been little reason to have faith that the civil liberties of people in this country would be protected in the atmosphere of hysteria that followed 9/11 and continues to this day. At home there have been immigrant roundups, indefinite detentions, deportations, and unauthorized domestic spying. Abroad there have extrajudicial killings, torture, bombings, war, and military occupations.

Likewise, the trial of Sacco and Vanzetti began immediately after Memorial Day, a year and a half after the orgy of death and patriotism that was World War I, when the newspapers still vibrating with the roll of drums and the jingoist rhetoric.

Twelve days into the trial, the press reported that the bodies of three soldiers had been transferred from the battlefields of France to the city of Brockton, and that the whole town had turned out for a patriotic ceremony. All of this was in newspapers that members of the jury could read. Sacco was cross-examined by prosecutor Katzmann:

> QUESTION: Did you love this country in the last week of May, 1917?
> SACCO: That is pretty hard for me to say in one word, Mr. Katzmann.
> QUESTION: There are two words you can use, Mr. Sacco, *yes* or *no*. What one is it?
> SACCO: Yes
> QUESTION: And in order to show your love for this United States of America when she was about to call upon you to become a soldier you ran away to Mexico?

At the beginning of the trial, Judge Thayer (who, speaking to a golf acquaintance, had referred to the defendants during the trial as "those anarchist bastards") said to the jury: "Gentlemen, I call upon you to render this service here that you have been summoned to perform with the same spirit of patriotism, courage, and devotion to duty as was exhibited by our soldier boys across the seas."

The emotions evoked by a bomb that exploded at Attorney General Palmer's home during a time of war—like emotions set loose by the violence of 9/11—created an anxious atmosphere in which civil liberties were compromised.

Sacco and Vanzetti understood that whatever legal arguments their lawyers could come up with would not prevail against the reality of class injustice. Sacco told the court, on sentencing: "I know the sentence will be between two classes, the oppressed class and the rich class. . . . That is why I am here today on this bench, for having been of the oppressed class."

That viewpoint seems dogmatic, simplistic. Not all court decisions are explained by it. But, lacking a theory that fits all cases, Sacco's simple, strong view is surely a better guide to understanding the legal system than one which assumes a contest among equals based on an objective search for truth.

Vanzetti knew that legal arguments would not save them. Unless a million Americans were organized, he and his friend Sacco would die. Not words, but struggle. Not appeals, but demands. Not petitions to the governor, but takeovers of the factories. Not lubricating the machinery of a supposedly fair system to make it work better, but a general strike to bring the machinery to a halt.

That never happened. Thousands demonstrated, marched, protested, not just in New York City, Boston, Chicago, San Francisco, but in London, Paris, Buenos Aires, South Africa. It wasn't enough. On the night of their execution, thousands demonstrated in Charlestown, but were kept away from the prison by a huge assembly of police. Protesters were arrested. Machine guns were on the rooftops and great searchlights swept the scene.

A great crowd assembled in Union Square on August 23, 1927. A few minutes after midnight, prison lights dimmed as the two men were electrocuted. The *New York World* described the scene: "The crowd responded with a giant sob. Women fainted in fifteen or twenty places. Others, too overcome, dropped to the curb and buried their heads in their hands. Men leaned on one anothers' shoulders and wept."

Their ultimate crime was their anarchism, an idea that today still startles us like a bolt of lightning because of its essential truth: we are all one, national boundaries and national hatreds must disappear, war is intolerable, the fruits of the earth must be shared, and only through organized struggle against authority can such a world come about.

What comes to us today from the case of Sacco and Vanzetti is not just tragedy, but inspiration. Their English was not perfect, but when they spoke it was a kind of poetry. Vanzetti said of his friend Sacco:

> Sacco is a heart, a faith, a character, a man; a man lover of nature and mankind. A man who gave all, who sacrifice all to the cause of liberty and to his love for mankind: money, rest, mundane ambition, his own wife, his children, himself and his own life. . . . Oh yes, I may be more witful, as some have put it, I am a better babbler than he is, but many, many times, in hearing his heartful voice ring a faith sublime, in considering his supreme sacrifice, remembering his heroism I felt small, small at the presence of his greatness, and found myself compelled to fight back from my eyes the tears, quench my heart throbbing to my throat to not weep before him—this man called chief and assassin and doomed.

Worst of all, they were anarchists, meaning they had some crazy notion of a full democracy in which neither foreignness nor poverty would exist, and thought that without these provocations war among nations would end for all time. But for this to happen the rich would have to be fought and their riches confiscated. That anarchist idea is a crime much worse than robbing a payroll, and so to this day the story of Sacco and Vanzetti cannot be recalled without great anxiety.

Sacco wrote to his son Dante: "So son, instead of crying, be strong, so as to be able to comfort your mother . . . take her for a long walk in the quiet country, gathering wild flowers here and there, resting under the shade of trees. . . . But remember always, Dante, in this play of happiness, don't you use all for yourself only . . . help the persecuted and the victim because they are your better friends. . . . In this struggle of life you will find more love and you will be loved."

Yes, it was their anarchism, their love for humanity, which doomed them. When Vanzetti was arrested, he had a leaflet in his pocket advertising a meeting to take place in five days. It is a leaflet that could be distributed today, all over the world, as appropriate now as it was the day of their arrest. It read:

> You have fought all the wars. You have worked for all the capitalists. You have wandered over all the countries. Have you harvested the fruits of your labors, the price of your victories? Does the past comfort you? Does the present smile on you? Does the future promise you anything? Have you found a piece of land where you can live like a human being and die like a human being? On these questions, on this argument, and on this theme, the struggle for existence, Bartolomeo Vanzetti will speak.

That meeting did not take place. But their spirit still exists today with people who believe and love and struggle all over the world.

35

THE OPTIMISM OF
UNCERTAINTY

I n this world of war and injustice, how does a person manage to stay socially engaged, committed to the struggle,
and remain healthy without burning out or becoming
resigned or cynical?

I am totally confident not that the world will get better,
but that we should not give up the game before all the
cards have been played. The metaphor is deliberate; life is
a gamble. Not to play is to foreclose any chance of winning.
To play, to act, is to create at least a possibility of chang-
ing the world.

There is a tendency to think that what we see in the present moment will continue. We forget how often we have
been astonished by the sudden crumbling of institutions, by
extraordinary changes in people's thoughts, by unexpected
eruptions of rebellion against tyrannies, by the quick collapse of systems of power that seemed invincible.

What leaps out from the history of the past hundred
years is its utter unpredictability. A revolution to overthrow
the czar of Russia in that most sluggish of semifeudal
empires not only startled the most advanced imperial powers but took Lenin himself by surprise and sent him rushing
by train to Petrograd. Who would have predicted the
bizarre shifts of World War II—the Nazi-Soviet pact (those
embarrassing photos of von Ribbentrop and Molotov shak-

ing hands), and the German army rolling through Russia, apparently invincible, causing colossal casualties, being turned back at the gates of Leningrad, on the western edge of Moscow, in the streets of Stalingrad, followed by the defeat of the German army, with Hitler huddled in his Berlin bunker, waiting to die?

And then the postwar world, taking a shape no one could have drawn in advance: The Chinese Communist revolution, the tumultuous and violent Cultural Revolution, and then another turnabout, with post-Mao China renouncing its most fervently held ideas and institutions, making overtures to the West, cuddling up to capitalist enterprise, perplexing everyone.

No one foresaw the disintegration of the old Western empires happening so quickly after the war, or the odd array of societies that would be created in the newly independent nations, from the benign village socialism of Nyerere's Tanzania to the madness of Idi Amin's adjacent Uganda. Spain became an astonishment. I recall a veteran of the Abraham Lincoln Brigade telling me that he could not imagine Spanish Fascism being overthrown without another bloody war. But after Franco was gone, a parliamentary democracy came into being, open to Socialists, Communists, anarchists, everyone.

The end of World War II left two superpowers with their respective spheres of influence and control, vying for military and political power. Yet they were unable to control events, even in those parts of the world considered to be their respective spheres of influence. The failure of the Soviet Union to have its way in Afghanistan, its decision to withdraw after almost a decade of ugly intervention, was the most striking evidence that even the possession of thermonuclear weapons does not guarantee domination over a determined population.

The United States has faced the same reality. It waged a full-scale war in Indochina, conducting the most brutal bombardment of a tiny peninsula in world history, and yet was forced to withdraw. In the headlines every day we see other instances of the failure of the presumably powerful over the presumably powerless, as in Bolivia and Brazil, where grassroots movements of workers and the poor have elected new presidents pledged to fight destructive corporate power.

Looking at this catalogue of huge surprises, it's clear that the struggle for justice should never be abandoned because of the apparent overwhelming power of those who have the guns and the money and who seem invincible in their determination to hold on to it. That apparent power has, again and again, proved vulnerable to human qualities less measurable than bombs and dollars: moral fervor, determination, unity, organization, sacrifice, wit, ingenuity, courage, patience—whether by blacks in Alabama and South Africa, peasants in El Salvador, Nicaragua, and Vietnam, or workers and intellectuals in Poland, Hungary, and the Soviet Union itself. No cold calculation of the balance of power need deter people who are persuaded that their cause is just.

I have tried hard to match my friends in their pessimism about the world (is it just my friends?), but I keep encountering people who, in spite of all the evidence of terrible things happening everywhere, give me hope. Wherever I go, I find such people, especially young people, in whom the future rests. And beyond the handful of activists there seem to be hundreds, thousands, more who are open to unorthodox ideas. But they tend not to know of one another's existence, and so, while they persist, they do so with the desperate patience of Sisyphus endlessly pushing the boulder up the mountain. I try to tell each group that they are not alone, and that the very people who are disheartened by the absence of a national movement are themselves proof of the potential for such a movement.

Revolutionary change does not come as one cataclysmic moment (beware of such moments!) but as an endless succession of surprises, moving zigzag toward a more decent society. We don't have to engage in grand, heroic actions to participate in the process of change. Small acts, when multiplied by millions of people, can quietly become a power no government can suppress, a power than can transform the world.

Even when we don't "win," there is fun and fulfillment in the fact that we have been involved, with other good people, in something worthwhile. We need hope. An optimist isn't necessarily a blithe, slightly sappy whistler in the dark of our time. To be hopeful in bad times is not being foolishly romantic. It is based on the fact that human history is a history not only of competition and cruelty but also of compassion, sacrifice, courage, kindness.

What we choose to emphasize in this complex history will determine our lives. If we see only the worst, it destroys our capacity to do something. If we remember those times and places—and there are so many—where people have behaved magnificently, it energizes us to act, and raises at least the possibility of sending this spinning top of a world in a different direction. And if we do act, in however small a way, we don't have to wait for some grand utopian future. The future is an infinite succession of presents, and to live now as we think human beings should live, in defiance of all that is bad around us, is itself a marvelous victory.

CREDITS AND PERMISSIONS

Howard Zinn, Introduction to David Cortright, *Soldiers in Revolt: GI Resistance During the Vietnam War*, updated edition (Chicago: Haymarket Books 2005). Copyright © 2005 by Howard Zinn. Reprinted by permission of Haymarket Books.

Howard Zinn, Introduction to Kathy Emery, *People Make Movements: Lessons from Freedom Summer* (Monroe: Common Courage Press). Copyright © 2006 by Howard Zinn. Reprinted by permission of Common Courage Press.

Howard Zinn, Introduction to Deepa Fernandes, *Targeted: Homeland Security and the Business of Immigration* (New York: Seven Stories Press 2006). Copyright © 2006 by Howard Zinn. Reprinted by permission of Seven Stories Press.

Howard Zinn, Introduction to Henry D. Thoreau, *The Higher Law: Thoreau on Civil Disobedience and Reform*, ed. Wendell Glick (Princeton: Princeton University Press 1973, 2004). Copyright © 2004 by Howard Zinn. Reprinted by permission of Princeton University Press.

Howard Zinn, Afterword to Zoe Trodd, *American Protest Literature* (Cambridge, MA: Harvard University Press). Copyright © 2006 by the President and Fellows of Harvard College.

BIBLIOGRAPHY

Gar Alperovitz, *The Decision to Use the Atomic Bomb* (Knopf, 1995).

Cesare Beccaria, *An Essay on Crimes and Punishments*, new ed. (Branden Books, 1983).

William Bradford, *Bradford's History of Plymouth Plantation, 1606-1646* (Adamant Media Corporation, 2001).

Tom Brokaw, *The Greatest Generation* (Random House, 1998).

Rachel Carson, *Silent Spring*, 40th Anniversary ed. (Mariner Books, 2002).

Rachel Carson, *The Sea Around Us*, rev. ed. (The Limited Editions Club, 1980).

David Cortright, *Soldiers in Revolt: GI Resistance During the Vietnam War*, updated edition (Haymarket Books, 2005).

Charles Dickens, *Hard Times* (St. Martin's Press, 2006).

Kathy Emery, *People Make Movements: Lessons from Freedom Summer* (Common Courage Press, [forthcoming]).

Jodie Evans, Mark LeVine, Viggo Mortensen, *Twilight of Empire: Responses to Occupation* (Perceval Press, 2004).

Paul Farmer, *Infections and Inequalities: The Modern Plagues* (University of California, 1999).

Howard Fast, *The Proud and the Free*, rpt. ed. (I Books, 2003).

Paul Fussell, *Wartime: Understanding and Behavior in the Second World War*, new ed. (Oxford University Press, USA, 1990).

Jean Giraudoux, *The Trojan War Will Not Take Place*, 3d, rev. ed. (Methuen, 1983).

Daniel Hallin, *The "Uncensored War": The Media and Vietnam*, rpt. ed. (University of California Press, 1989).

Joseph Heller, *Catch-22*, rpt. ed. (Simon & Schuster, 1996).

John Hersey, *Hiroshima*, rpt. ed. (Vintage, 1989).

Richard Hofstadter, *The American Political Tradition* (Vintage Books, 1948).

David M. Kennedy, *Freedom from Fear: The American People in Depression and War, 1929–1945*, new ed. (Oxford University Press, USA, 2001).

Merriam-Webster's Collegiate Dictionary, 11th Edition (Merriam-Webster, 2003).

Peter Novick, *The Holocaust in American Life* (Houghton Mifflin, 1999).

Michael Ondaatje, *The English Patient*, rpt. ed. (Vintage, 1993).

George Orwell, *1984* (Signet Classics, 1950).

Thomas Paine, *Common Sense* (Signet Classics, 2003).

Ray Raphael, *A People's History of the American Revolution* (New Press, 2001).

Michael Scheuer, *Imperial Hubris: Why The West Is Losing The War On Terror*, new ed. (Potomac Books, 2005).

Ignazio Silone, *Fontamara*, new ed. (Everyman's Library, 1994).

Upton Sinclair, *Boston: A Novel* (Classic Publishers, 1999).

Upton Sinclair, *The Jungle*, new ed. (See Sharp Press, 2003).

John Steinbeck, *The Grapes of Wrath*, Steinbeck Centennial ed. (Penguin, 2002).

Gino Strada, *Green Parrots: A War Surgeon's Diary* (Charta, 2005).

Dalton Trumbo, *Johnny Got His Gun*, rpt. ed. Citadel Press, 1994).

Lao Tsu, *Tao Te Ching*, 25th Anniversary ed. (Vintage, 1997).

Mark Twain, *A Connecticut Yankee in King Arthur's Court* as included in, *The Best Short Works of Mark Twain* (Enriched Classics, 2004).

Carl Van Doren, *Mutiny in January: The story of a crisis in the Continental army now for the first time fully told from many hitherto unknown or neglected sources, both American and British* (Viking, 1943; rpt. ed., Augustus M. Kelley, 1973).

Voltaire, *Candide* (Penguin, 1977).

Kurt Vonnegut, *Slaughterhouse Five* (Laurel, 1991).

Kurt Vonnegut, *Cat's Cradle* (Dial Press, 1998).

Kurt Vonnegut, *Timequake*, rpt. ed. (Berkley Trade, 1998).

Richard Wright, *Black Boy* (Harper Perennial Modern Classics, 1998).

Malcolm X, *The Autobiography of Malcolm X: As Told to Alex Haley*, reissued ed. (Ballantine Books, 1987).

Howard Zinn, *A People's History of the United States* (Harper Perennial Modern Classics, 2005).

INDEX

The Rights and Duties of the
Individual in Relation to
Government Thoreau, 125
The Sea Around Us (Carson), 238
Thoreau, Henry David
assessment of, 121
on invasion of Mexico (1846),
121
jailing of, 122, 224–25
on nations, 155
on power of voting, 136
writings of, 121
Tilden, Samuel, 63–64
Timequake (Vonnegut), 241
Tirin Kot, killings in, 80
Togo, mediated end of war sought
by, 52–53
Tokyo, firebombing of, 89, 103
Tolstoy, Leo, 133
Tor Tul, on bombings of Madoo,
Afghanistan, 82
Tora Bora, Afghanistan, bombing
of, 86–87
Torai village, bombing of, 83–84
Trail of Tears, deaths during, 58
Tran Khanh Tuyet, 216
Transcontinental railroad, con-
struction of, 250
Treaties, Article VI of the
Constitution, 164
The Trojan War Will Not Take Place
(Giraudoux), 154
Truman, Harry, 202
Trumbo, Dalton, 24, 239
Truth
power of, 16
tenacity of, 23
Tulsa massacre, 101
Turkey Shoot, Iraqi deaths in, 89
Twain, Mark, 58, 113, 115

*See also A Connecticut Yankee in
King Arthur's Court* (Twain)
Twilight of Empire, 182

UN World Food Programme, on
child starvation, 209
*The Uncensored War: The Media and
Vietnam* (Hallin), 131
Unconditional surrender principle,
54
Underground Railroad, 128
Union Maids (documentary), 247
United Fruit. *See* Cuba, invasion of
United Nations, establishment of,
19
United States
becoming a humanitarian
superpower, 94–95
class differences within, 42
divisions within, 36
infant mortality in, 205
poverty rate in, 205
reaction to September 11 terrorist attacks, 93
as unique, 143–144
worldwide military presence of,
151
United States expansionism, 92
Universal humanism, 109
U.S. armed forces, disobedience
during Vietnam War, 137
U.S. history, ignorance of, 183
U.S. military budget, 23
U.S. military policies, and radicalization of Islamic world, 90
U.S. National Intelligence
Estimate, on terrorism,
194–195

ABOUT THE AUTHOR

Howard Zinn grew up in the immigrant slums of Brooklyn where he worked in shipyards in his late teens. He saw combat duty as a U.S. Air Force bombardier in World War II. Afterward he received his doctorate in history from Columbia University and was a postdoctoral Fellow in East Asian Studies at Harvard University. His first book, *LaGuardia in Congress*, was an Albert Beveridge Prize winner. He is the author of numerous books, including his epic masterpiece, *A People's History of the United States*, "a brilliant and moving history of the American people from the point of view of those who have been exploited politically and economically and whose plight has been largely omitted from most histories" (*Library Journal*). A professor emeritus of political science at Boston University, Zinn lives with his wife, Roslyn, in the Boston area, near their children and grandchildren.